MAY 1 5 2006

S0-AZT-387

WITHDRAWN

PROPERTY OF
Kankakee Public Library

People to Know

# Bob Dylan
## The Life and Times of an American Icon

Michael A. Schuman

**Enslow Publishers, Inc.**

| | |
|---|---|
| 40 Industrial Road | PO Box 38 |
| Box 398 | Aldershot |
| Berkeley Heights, NJ 07922 | Hants GU12 6BP |
| USA | UK |

http://www.enslow.com

Copyright © 2003 by Michael A. Schuman

All rights reserved.

No part of this book may be reproduced by any means
without the written permission of the publisher.

**Library of Congress Cataloging-in-Publication Data**

Schuman, Michael.
    Bob Dylan : the life and times of an American icon / by Michael A. Schuman.
      p. cm. — (People to know)
    Summary: Profiles Bob Dylan, a singer and songwriter for over forty years who is
known for such songs as "Blowin' in the Wind," "Just like a Woman," and "Things
Have Changed," the Academy Award winning song from the film, "Wonder Boys."
    Includes bibliographical references (p.   ) and index.
    Discography: p.
    ISBN 0-7660-2108-4
    1. Dylan, Bob, 1941—-Juvenile literature. 2. Rock musicians—United States—
Biography—Juvenile literature. [1. Dylan, Bob, 1941- 2. Musicians. 3. Rock music.]
I. Title. II. Series.
    ML3930.D97S34  2003
    782.42164'092—dc21

                                   2003002482

Printed in the United States of America

10 9 8 7 6 5 4 3 2 1

**To Our Readers:**
We have done our best to make sure all Internet Addresses in this book were active
and appropriate when we went to press. However, the author and the publisher have
no control over and assume no liability for the material available on those Internet
sites or on other Web sites they may link to. Any comments or suggestions can be sent
by e-mail to comments@enslow.com or to the address on the back cover.

Every effort has been made to locate all copyright holders of material used in this
book. If any errors or omissions have occurred, corrections will be made in future
editions of this book.

**Illustration Credits:** Academy of Motion Picture Arts and Sciences, p. 87;
AP Worldwide, p. 79; Diana Davies, p. 49; Greg T. Jones, Skylite Studio, 9.
63; Hibbing Public Library, p. 23; Jimmy Carter Library, p. 71; John
Brassil, p. 93; Library of Congress, pp. 4, 13, 22 28, 33, 35, 38, 43, 47, 91;
University Archives, Department of Rare Books and Special Collections,
Princeton University Library, p. 76; Zimmy's & The Atrium Restaurant,
p. 14.

**Cover Illustration:** AP Worldwide

**3 1558 00224 1594**

# Contents

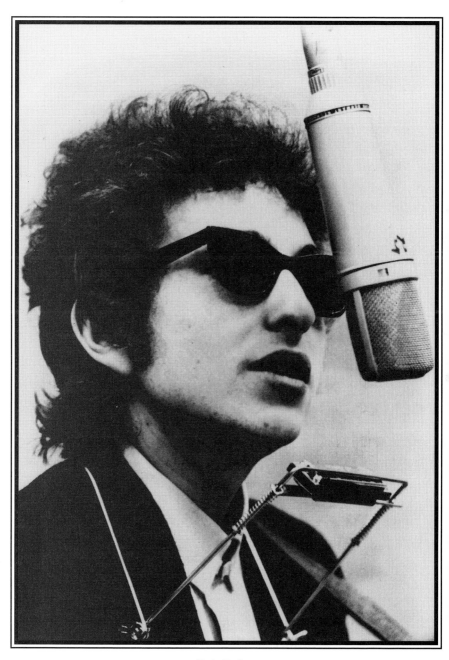

*Bob Dylan*

# Passing the Basket

Bob Dylan was just one of many faceless New York City folk singers in the winter of 1960. He had just arrived from Minnesota with a guitar and the hope of a music career.

As soon as Dylan arrived in the big city, he knew just where to go. The section of New York City known as Greenwich Village had long drawn artists, writers, and musicians. Poet and author Edgar Allen Poe, author Theodore Dreiser, composer Aaron Copland, artist Jackson Pollock, and comedian Bill Cosby all had worked in Greenwich Village.

It did not take long for Dylan to make friends. He told people he met that he was a struggling folk singer and could not afford a place of his own. Many allowed him to stay in their homes.

Dylan knew that the only place an unknown like himself could start was at the bottom. There were several clubs in Greenwich Village, most centered around bustling MacDougal Street, where beginning musicians played for almost nothing. They did not receive a paycheck from club owners. Instead, baskets were passed through the audience for any money the crowd wished to donate. Mostly, they gave little more than pocket change.

At this early stage of Dylan's career, there was something just as important as money: exposure. By playing these small, crowded, smoke-filled rooms, Dylan and others hoped managers of larger clubs would see them and sign them to play.

One club Dylan played early was the Café Wha? at 115 MacDougal Street. Since evening and night shows were reserved for proven professionals, Dylan performed for free in the afternoon. He sang folk numbers like "Barbara Allen" and a selection of tunes made famous by a folk legend named Woody Guthrie. Now and then the Jewish-born Dylan would also work into his repertoire the traditional Jewish folk song "Hava Nagila." Dylan became known for putting offbeat humor in his routines, mocking widely accepted middle–class attitudes and ideas. He would subtly put down people who were not folk music fans but who came to Greenwich Village from suburbs to see singers they basically considered oddities. Dylan was also noted for his unusual voice, which was described at different times as tinny, whiny, metallic, nasal, and twangy. One folk singer said it was like "a dog with his leg caught in barbed wire."[1]

Dylan's unconventional appearance was something else altogether. Often seen strolling around Greenwich Village wearing a long winter coat and a black corduroy hat, Dylan was said to resemble everything from an eastern European immigrant to a character out of a Charles Dickens novel.

Some entertainers are willing to wait ten years or longer to be discovered. But Dylan was not like other entertainers. In the late summer of 1961, he learned that a folk-singing friend named Carolyn Hester had a recording session scheduled with a major company, Columbia Records. Overseeing the session would be an important record producer named John Hammond, Sr. Hammond had discovered legends of big band jazz who had been immensely popular in the 1930s and 1940s. These included Benny Goodman, Count Basie, and Billie Holiday. Now he was turning his attention to the fashionable folk scene.

Dylan asked Hester if he could play background harmonica during her session, and she agreed. He was thrilled. Dylan first met Hammond at a rehearsal on September 14 and Hammond was impressed with Dylan's playing. They would meet again on September 29 for the actual recording session.

Dylan then took another bold step in advancing his career. Bursting with confidence, he placed a phone call to Robert Shelton, music editor of *The New York Times*. *The Times* is one of the most highly regarded newspapers in the United States. Dylan asked Shelton to come hear him perform at Gerde's Folk City.

Most critics refuse to become personally involved

with those they review. If critics become friendly with a performer, there may be less chance they will be objective in discussing his or her act. Dylan took a risk making that call. It was possible that Shelton would be angry for this pip-squeak songster telling him how to do his job.

But Shelton agreed to hear Dylan sing. The critic was well known in the folk singing community of Greenwich Village and was willing to hear a new act.

Now that Dylan had attracted a critic's attention, there was another risk. It was one thing to have confidence to make that risky phone call. But he needed something else: talent. What if Shelton hated his performance? Shelton's words would be printed in the pages of a hugely important newspaper.

Dylan opened the evening of September 26 for a more established folk act called the Greenbriar Boys. But to the readers of the September 29 edition of *The New York Times*, it appeared the young singer from Minnesota was the true star. The newspaper headline read, "Bob Dylan: A Distinctive Stylist." The club's feature act appeared in smaller print under the main headline. It read, "Greenbriar Boys Are Also on Bill With Bluegrass Music." Shelton wrote of Dylan, "His clothes may need a bit of tailoring, but when he works his guitar, harmonica or piano and composes new songs faster than he can remember them, there is no doubt that he is bursting at the seams with talent."[2]

When Dylan showed up for Hester's recording session at the Columbia Records studios later that day, he handed Hammond a copy of the newspaper with the glowing review. Hammond was impressed and seemed to spend much of the recording session paying more attention to Dylan than to Hester.

There are different stories about what happened next. An often-told tale is that Hammond offered Dylan his own recording contract on the spot. Others say that Hammond made Dylan audition, or try out, for a recording contract. What is definitely known is that on October 26, 1961, Dylan was sent his first recording contract. It stated that Dylan would record only for Columbia Records for the next five years. If his first record sold poorly, Columbia could drop the contract. From whatever money his records earned, Dylan would be given a 2 percent royalty of those earnings. In other words, if a record earned one dollar for Columbia, Dylan would receive two cents.[3]

It was not much. But it was a start.

# The Rocking Golden Chords

$B$ob Dylan was born the night of May 24, 1941, in St. Mary's Hospital in Duluth, Minnesota. His real name is Robert Allen Zimmerman. He would not become known as Bob Dylan for nineteen years.

Duluth is a small city of about 85,000 people on the shore of Lake Superior, the biggest of the Great Lakes. Many in Duluth make their livings in jobs relating to the shipping business. Numerous others earn money by working in iron mines of the nearby eastern Mesabi Range. The region is so well known for its iron ranges that the people here are known as rangers.

Dylan's father, Abram Zimmerman, worked for the Standard Oil Company. Abram was a serious and practical man. He joined Standard Oil as a messenger at sixteen and worked his way up to the position of junior supervisor.

Abe's wife Beatrice, nicknamed Beatty, liked to keep busy. If she was not working a part-time job such as selling clothes in a department store, she could often be found volunteering at the local chapter of Hadassah, an organization promoting good will and education among Jews.

The Zimmermans were practicing Jews living in a place where there was not a huge Jewish population. Most residents of Duluth were Lutherans of Scandinavian ancestry. There was also a sizable number of Catholics with eastern European roots. Still, there were enough Jews to support four synagogues, and according to a local historian named Joseph Papo, there was no open bigotry toward Jews.[1]

Even as a toddler, Bobby liked to sing for people. When he was three, his father took him to work where the curly-haired child stood atop his father's desk and sang into a recording machine called a Dictaphone. A group of Abe's fellow employees gathered around, listened, and applauded when the boy finished his song.

A little over a year later, Bobby gave a public performance at a Mother's Day celebration in town. At first, the gathered crowd seemed uninterested. So Bobby stamped his foot on the stage and called out, "If everybody in this room will keep quiet, I will sing for my grandmother. I'm going to sing 'Some Sunday Morning.'"[2]

His mother Beatty recalled, "Well, he sang it, and

they [the audience] tore the place apart. They clapped so hard that he sang his other big number, [a then popular show tune called] 'Accentuate the Positive.' He didn't know much more than those two songs. Our phone never stopped ringing with people congratulating me."[3]

The Zimmermans did not stay long in Duluth. After World War II ended in late summer of 1945, the mining and shipping businesses slowed down. Abe was soon laid off at Standard Oil. The Zimmermans had another mouth to feed as Bobby's brother, David Benjamin Zimmerman, was born in February 1946. In addition, Abe suffered from a disability, which made it hard to find work.

Years later, Bob said, "My father was a very active man, but he was stricken very early by an attack of polio [an illness causing the loss of use of one's muscles]. The illness put an end to all his dreams, I believe. He could barely walk. When we moved from the north of the country two of his brothers who were electrical fitters opened a shop and they took him with them so he could mind the shop."[4]

The shop was about seventy miles east of Duluth in the mining town of Hibbing, Minnesota where Abe and Beatty had lived years earlier. Being smaller than Duluth, Hibbing also had fewer Jews. But Beatty said they were friendly with the Catholics and Lutherans who lived in Hibbing and often attended each other's parties.

The Zimmerman family moved into an apartment next to Alice School where Bob attended first grade. Bob found his first day confusing. When the bell rang

*Bob Zimmerman and his family moved to Hibbing, Minnesota, in 1947. This picture of downtown was taken around the same time.*

for recess, he thought it meant the end of the school day so he went home. Once he learned how long the school day was, he settled in with no problem.

Within a year, Bob's family moved into their own house at the corner of Seventh Avenue and Twenty-fifth Street. Abe kept busy at the shop while Beatty took a part time job as a salesperson in a department store. Often Bobby's parents were not home when he returned from school, so he would head straight to his bedroom and listen to his radio or record player. Bobby had a huge collection of small records known as 45s, short for 45 rpm, because they spin at forty-five revolutions per minute. Unlike today's compact discs, or even long-playing record albums, 45s had only one song on each side. They were more popular then than albums, and kids collected them to hear their favorite songs without waiting until they were played on the radio.

When he was about ten, Bobby wrote a lengthy and creative poem for Beatty for Mother's Day. The last stanza went:

> *My dear mother, I hope that you*
> *Will never grow old and gray,*
> *So that all the people in the world will say:*
> *'Hello, young lady, Happy Mother's Day.'*
> *Love, Bobby*[5]

The next month he wrote a similar poem for his father, which ended:

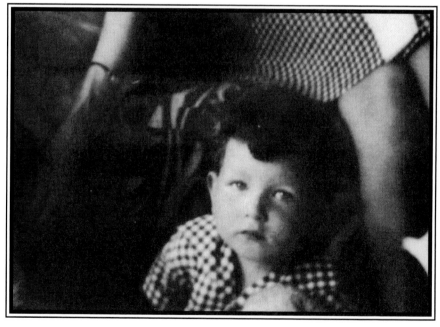

*Even as a toddler Bobby Zimmerman liked to sing for people.*

*I'm very lucky to have a dad this good*
*And if all the other kids only could,*
*You just can't beat him at any cost.*
*And without my dad, I'd be very lost.*
*Happy Father's Day. Love Bobby.*"[6]

At age twelve, Bob began lessons for his bar mitzvah, a ceremony marking a Jewish boy reaching the age when he is responsible to observe God's commandments. Jewish girls have a similar ceremony called a bat mitzvah. A bar or bat mitzvah is a very important event, usually including a long religious service followed by a huge party. When the big day came, Bob, then thirteen, stood at the altar and chanted the same Hebrew prayers that Jews have been saying for thousands of years. Between his rabbi's instruction and Bobby's talent, guests agreed the youngster did a superb job. After the religious service, around four hundred friends and relatives of the Zimmermans capped off the day by attending a gala party in the ballroom of one of Hibbing's finest hotels.

It was not always like Bob to be the center of attention. In school he was quiet and never had much to say. At home he spent time making up tunes on the family piano or writing poetry and drawing pictures alone in his bedroom. Although he had a few close friends, he felt he had different interests than most kids his age.

He never tired of listening to the radio. The biggest station in Hibbing, WMFG, played mainstream pop music. At the time that consisted of pleasant but not innovative songs. Many were sung by vocalists such as Doris Day and Perry Como who had been with the famous big bands of the 1940s. Bobby found much of it boring.

At night, when many smaller stations went off the air, Bobby was able to pick up radio stations from cities and towns hundreds of miles away in the lower Mississippi River Valley. They played country music, which at the time was called country and western. Bobby's favorite country singer was Hank Williams, one of the greatest of all time. Williams told stories in his songs about heartache and lost love with titles such as "I'm So Lonesome I Could Cry" and "Your Cheating Heart." Bobby was intrigued at how Williams could emit strong feelings of loneliness in his songs.

But Williams led a short and tragic life. He fought an alcohol addiction that began when he was a teenager and died of an alcohol-related heart attack on New Year's Day, 1953. He was just twenty-nine years old.

Along with Hank Williams, Dylan was very impressed by a popular singer named Johnny Ray. Like Williams, Ray sang about broken hearts and unanswered love. Two of Ray's best-known songs were, "Cry" and "The Little White Cloud That Cried." Ray put so much emotion into his songs that some fans said his music brought them to tears. People who did not know that he was white heard his soul-stirring delivery and thought he must be African American. Dylan said Johnny Ray was "the first singer whose voice and style I totally fell in love with."[7]

In addition to music, Bobby loved movies. His

grandfather and uncle owned two of Hibbing's biggest theaters, and every week Bobby would lose himself in the fantasy world of the movie screen.

One film in 1955 caught Bobby's attention. It was titled *Rebel Without a Cause*, starring a young actor named James Dean who played a troubled teenager. Unlike many similar movies, this one portrayed Dean's character, Jimmy Stark, sympathetically. Two other teen characters were treated similarly. Their parents meant well but were out of touch and unable to help their kids. The three main characters felt alienated from their fellow teens as much as their parents.

Bobby saw a lot of himself in Jimmy Stark. Bobby's parents tried their best but did not seem to understand the budding artist Bobby was becoming. Bobby was so taken by James Dean's character that he started dressing like him. Almost overnight, he shunned the dressy school clothes his mother had picked out for him and bought for himself some Levis, a motorcycle jacket, and a pair of biker's boots.

In 1955, rock and roll was a new type of music starting to catch on among young people. Hibbing's WMFG would not play it, but at night Bobby's radio picked up powerful stations from Louisiana and Arkansas playing a style of music called rhythm and blues. It was a combination of traditional African-American blues and jazz with a strong backbeat, and at first it was performed almost entirely by African-American musicians and singers. White artists such as Pat Boone and Georgia Gibbs recorded softer, watered-down versions of the same songs.

Some white teens including Bobby liked the rougher, louder, and harsher original rhythm and blues renditions. One of his favorite artists was Little Richard, a flamboyant African-American pianist and singer from Macon, Georgia, originally named Richard Penniman. Little Richard sang and screamed his songs, known for raucous rhythms, hot piano, untamed saxophone solos, and lyrics filled with sexual undertones.

One of Bobby's friends, John Bucklin, remembered Bobby's first impression of this music. Bucklin related, "He couldn't believe it. The two of us were so hungry for anything, it didn't matter what it was, and then this sound comes along and sweeps us off our feet. We knew we were onto something that nobody else in Hibbing had any idea about—something very special—even though, at the time, we still weren't sure what it all meant."[8]

Bob tried to find ways to further explore rhythm and blues. It was not easy in mainly white Hibbing. Bob learned that in a nearby town called Virginia lived an African-American disc jockey named James Reese, who played rhythm and blues music for a small private radio station. Bobby became friends with Reese and the disc jockey taught Bobby much about rhythm and blues.

Bob decided this music would become his life's work. With three other Hibbing teens, he organized a rock and roll band called the Golden Chords. With Bob on piano, they practiced hard and planned to show off their musical abilities at a high school talent show in March 1958. Almost the entire student body of roughly 1,500 students, along with the faculty, was on hand. Student performers included a magic act, a pantomime artist, and classical musicians.

Then it was time for the Golden Chords. Nobody could have foreseen what would happen next.

The band played rock-and-roll music so loud it was a wonder the school building did not shake. The audience found it hard to believe that shy, quiet Bobby Zimmerman was singing like a white Little Richard. Indeed, many had never heard of Little Richard, and thought Bob was acting like a crazy person. Some of the students laughed at the music and thought the band looked silly. Others reveled in the new jarring sound.

One thing was for sure—Bobby Zimmerman was no longer viewed as the bashful kid who never spoke in class. He was the reigning rock and roller of Hibbing, Minnesota.

The Golden Chords did not win the talent show. The pantomime artist did. The teachers and school staff decided the music was too loud for Hibbing High School and banned rock and roll from future talent shows.

# Nights in Dinkytown

Shortly after Bob found he could rock the house, he also discovered girls. Bob dated several from his school, including a pretty blonde named Judy Rubin. Bob and Judy also spent several summers together at Camp Herzl, a Jewish overnight camp in Wisconsin.

But his first serious girlfriend was a slender, pale blonde with the poetic name of Echo Star Helstrom. Unlike Bob, Echo was not Jewish and was from a poor family. Her differences from him seemed to make her more attractive. Bob's brother David said, "Bobby always went with the daughters of miners, farmers, and workers in Hibbing. He just found them a lot more interesting."[1]

Bob and Echo enjoyed each other's company. One

of their favorite activities was meeting after school and walking to a small restaurant called the L&B Luncheonette, where they listened to their favorite songs on the jukebox and talked.

Like Jimmy Stark in *Rebel Without a Cause*, Bob was rebelling against his family's middle-class background and values. By the late 1950s, Hibbing's iron ore supply had been nearly depleted and the town's mines were laying off workers. Out of work miners had trouble paying their bills. Meanwhile, the Zimmerman Brothers bought the store they had previously only worked at. They expanded into a larger space and began selling furniture as well as appliances. It became known as Zimmerman Electric and Furniture.

When people could not pay for the items they bought, the furniture or appliances had to be repossessed, or taken back by the store. According to service manager Benny Orlando, the Zimmerman brothers were very patient with people who could not pay their bills. He said, "The Zimmermans really leaned over backwards for a lot of people, they let it go right to the end."[2] But Bob looked down on his father for repossessing the belongings of out-of-work people. He felt his father lacked compassion for his customers down on their luck.[3]

Abe never held his son's feelings against him. He bought Bob a used car, then a Harley-Davidson motorcycle. One afternoon Bob and a friend named Leroy Hoikkala were riding their motorcycles along nearby tracks when they stopped to let a freight train pass. Just after the train went by, Bob took off, not

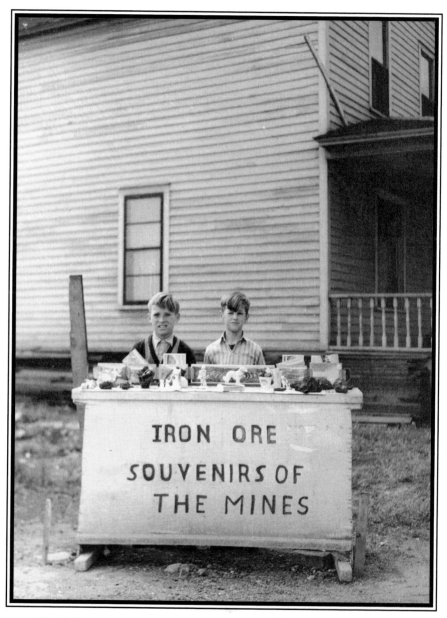

*Until the 1950s a large percentage of Hibbing's economy came from the iron mines. This photograph was taken in Hibbing in 1941, the year Dylan was born.*

realizing that another train was charging down the tracks from the opposite direction. There was no time to stop, but Bob skidded out of control and over-turned his bike just past the tracks, less than a foot from the charging train. Amazingly, he survived without injury.

When not on his motorcycle or in school Bob was often found playing with the Golden Chords. They rehearsed regularly on Sunday afternoons in a restaurant named Collier's, and Hibbing's teenagers stopped by to hear them play songs made famous by rock pioneers such as Little Richard, Buddy Holly, Elvis Presley, and Gene Vincent. In time, Bob tired of piano and wanted to play a portable instrument. He took lessons from the Golden Chords' guitarist Monte Edwardson, and picked up the guitar quickly.

Bob soon bought his own guitar, a Silverstone acoustic for twenty five dollars from a music store in Hibbing. But he quickly grew tried of it and wanted something that would produce a wilder sound—something electric. So he scoured the music stores of Hibbing

*Bob Zimmerman spent his free time riding his motorcycle and practicing with his band, the Golden Chords, when he was a teenager.*

until he found a ramshackle shop run by an elderly Finnish man named Mr. Hautela. The old gentleman sold Bobby a black Ozark Supro electric guitar for sixty dollars, even though the high school rocker could not afford an amplifier. Bobby found a way around that problem. As he played the Ozark Supro in his bedroom, he pressed it against the window so the sound would vibrate and echo, causing a kind of fake amplifying effect.

In June 1959, Bob graduated high school. Listed underneath his senior picture in the school yearbook were his activities: Latin Club in his sophomore year, Social Studies Club in his senior year. His ambition, the yearbook editors wrote, was "To join Little Richard."[4]

Hooking up with one of his rock idols might have been his dream, but Bob's immediate plans were not so exciting. He split up with Echo and like many of his fellow Hibbing graduates, traveled downstate in the fall of 1959 to attend the University of Minnesota in the big city of St. Paul.

At college Bob attended freshman classes and moved into a Jewish fraternity house, Sigma Alpha Mu. Because the first letters of the three words in the fraternity's name spelled "SAM," its members were known as Sammies.

At times, Bob entertained his fraternity brothers with his piano playing. He tried to impress them by making outrageous boasts. He bragged that he had played with Little Richard and Buddy Holly. He also claimed to be Bobby Vee, a successful pop musician at the time who had several hit records. Whether they believed him is anyone's guess.

It was not long before Bob started losing interest in his classes and having less to do with his fraternity brothers. He still lived in the SAM house, but spent most of his time there alone in his room, just like he had growing up at home. His fraternity brothers began avoiding him, and Bob started to cut classes.

Although Bob had left Echo back in Hibbing, he discovered that his friend Judy Rubin lived across the street in a Jewish sorority, Sigma Delta Tau. They began seeing each other regularly. Bob also started to spend time in a part of St. Paul called Dinkytown. It was an area of small nightclubs and apartments which were home to young people known as beatniks. Beatniks generally rejected their parents' values and supported liberal political ideas. Beatniks considered themselves hip and others square.

Bob noticed that the beatniks in Dinkytown were ignoring rock and roll. Over the past two years, the music had changed greatly. For several reasons, many leading rock performers were out of the picture. Buddy Holly had died in an airplane crash. Little Richard quit music to become a minister. Elvis Presley was drafted into the Army. The current batch of rock-and-roll stars, including Paul Anka, Frankie Avalon, and Bobby Rydell were clean cut and anything but rebellious.

To beatniks, folk music was hip. Folk songs are like folk stories. They were originally passed from one generation to another long before they were written down. Folk had long been viewed as the music of struggling people. Modern folk music is written down but is sung and played in the style of traditional folk. That usually means a singer is accompanied only by an acoustic guitar.

In the early 1960s, electric guitars and drum sets were thought best for the more juvenile rock and roll. When born in the 1950s, rock music was seen as rebellious, and restless teenagers celebrated it. But by the early sixties, most rock songs were lightweight numbers about young love or new dance crazes. Some music historians refer to that time as rock's innocent days. More critical people say they were rock's empty period.

College students looked for music with more meaning, and they found it in folk music. Many of the most respected folk performers, such as Woody Guthrie, Pete Seeger, and the Weavers, had been active in very liberal causes. Some in mainstream America considered them ultra-liberal to the point of being un-American. They sang about working poor people, like hardscrabble farmers and the iron ore miners Bob had grown up with. Woody Guthrie's most famous song, "This Land is Your Land," was written to declare that all people, rich or poor, white or black, belonged in America.

Across the nation in neighborhoods like Dinkytown, coffeehouses and folk music clubs sprouted like dandelions in spring. Several were located in cellars of old buildings. The rule seemed to be the grungier the better. Bob took note of this trend. He got rid of his electric guitar and started playing a

Gibson acoustic one. Before long, he was singing in the coffeehouses and clubs of Dinkytown.

Somewhere around this time he decided that Bob Zimmerman was no name for an entertainer. He chose a new name for himself: Bob Dylan. Like much of Dylan's early life, the selection of his stage name is shrouded in mystery. Most Dylan historians say he chose the name in honor of a famous Welsh poet named Dylan Thomas.

Bob has never admitted anything of the kind. In fact, many times he flatly denied it. In one interview, he was asked if there was a link between his name and Dylan Thomas. Bob answered, "No, none at all! If I were a fan of Dylan Thomas I would have sung his poems or I would be called Bob Thomas."[5] One rock critic, Nat Hentoff, wrote that the name Dylan was close to the last name of one of his relatives who was a gambler.[6] Others have said he named himself after Matt Dillon, a character in a then-popular television western series, *Gunsmoke.*

Regardless of the reason, Bob Dylan was now the young singer/guitarist's name. He took a few gigs, or performing jobs, wherever he could. One night he might play at the Hillel House, home of a social group for Jewish students, while the next night he would perform at a Dinkytown club called the Ten O'Clock Scholar. It was not hard to get these gigs since just about anyone with a guitar and a repertoire of a few songs was allowed to play.

Bob's first influence as a folk singer was an African-American woman named Odetta Holmes, who sang under the name Odetta. She was about ten

*Folk-singer Odetta Holmes influenced Dylan at an early age. She is shown here at the March on Washington in 1963. She is on right with guitar.*

years older than Dylan, and was well known in folk clubs from San Francisco to New York. Odetta has a rich, throaty voice that she put to use singing protest songs, blues, and traditional African-American folk tunes. Dylan often played Odetta's best-known songs such as "Mule Skinner" and "Buked and Scorned" in his shows.

Often seated at a table near the front at Dylan's gigs was Judy Rubin, who would come to listen and offer encouragement. Much of the time she brought friends with her, and they would call out requests. Bob and Judy were falling in love with each other.

But Dylan had a dream that Judy was hesitant to

share with him. He was on the verge of dropping out of college to try to become a full-time singer and musician. Judy wanted a more traditional life without the ups and downs involved in a musician's risky career. Because of their differences, Judy and Bob broke up in 1960.

Dylan soon became friendly with a couple named Gretel Hoffman and David Whitaker. The three shared the same interests, including liberal political views, beat poets such as Allen Ginsberg and Gregory Corso, and folk and blues music. One day Whitaker suggested Dylan read a book called *Bound for Glory*, written by folk singer Woody Guthrie in 1943.

In the book, Guthrie tells how he traveled the United States hitchhiking and hopping trains. He writes glowingly of meeting good working people going through tough times and sharing the company of homeless people. Dylan was impressed how Guthrie championed the underprivileged through his writing and music. He identified with Guthrie and wanted to sing the praises of poor and struggling people, too.[7]

Dylan realized he was not going to achieve his dream in St. Paul. Yet he knew he was not ready for big entertainment centers such as San Francisco or New York. So after halfheartedly finishing his freshman year of college, Dylan quit school and moved to a city where folk music was just starting to catch on: Denver, Colorado.

He was hired to sing in a few clubs, but was not popular. Folk music had by now crossed over from the beatnik culture into the mainstream. Songs by respectable folk groups such has the Highwaymen, the Brothers Four, and the Kingston Trio were heard on radios across the country. Those who took folk music seriously looked down upon them. These artists ignored the likes of Woody Guthrie to sing safe folk standards such as "Michael Row the Boat Ashore" and "Tom Dooley." Dylan stuck to music that would have made Woody Guthrie proud—about poor and downtrodden people.

Dylan realized Denver was not for him. He tried playing a regular gig in a restaurant in a nearby historic mining town, Central City. It was popular with tourists who did not take folk music seriously— Dylan's or anyone else's. Dylan lasted a few days, then moved back to Denver. After a falling-out with his former roommates over some records they insisted he had stolen, Dylan felt it was time to leave. He arranged a ride with a man who was driving across the country. Accounts say Dylan arrived in New York City in either late 1960 or early 1961. In New York, Bob Dylan was going to do all he could to follow his dream.

# Meeting Woody

$A$side from making a name for himself, Dylan had one other goal in his early New York days. He wanted to meet Woody Guthrie. His Greenwich Village friends said that all Dylan ever talked about was "Goin' t'see Woody."[1]

At the time, Guthrie was living an hour from New York City in Greystone Park State Hospital in Morris Plains, New Jersey. Dylan's once rambunctious idol was wasting away from a rare condition called Huntington's Disease, which attacked his nervous system, causing slurred speech and uncontrollable tics. Gaunt and weak, Guthrie was only forty-nine but looked much older.

Dylan contacted the hospital and asked if he could visit Guthrie. One might have thought a folk legend would have no interest in meeting an unknown fan. Nowadays, it would be similar to a kid playing guitar in a high school garage band trying to meet Bruce Springsteen.

But surprisingly, Guthrie was happy to have a visitor. Perhaps Guthrie's willingness to meet the young folk singer stemmed from the fact that he had been a resident of the hospital since 1956. Maybe he was hungry for company, even if it was a much younger and unknown stranger. Some have said that Guthrie's openness to meet Dylan was due to his poor mental health. They report that Guthrie was so sick that he was not thinking rationally. In his condition, they say, he would have allowed anyone to visit him. However, the majority of Dylan historians disagree and say that although Guthrie's body was weak, his mind was as sharp as ever.

Guthrie recognized Dylan's talent and would often ask his caretakers when "the boy" would next be visiting. Dylan was ecstatic. In a letter home, he wrote, "Woody likes me—he tells me to sing for him—he's the greatest holiest godliest one in the world."[2] Dylan's friend Mark Spoelstra remembered about Dylan, "It was all he wanted to talk about. He'd just been to see him that first time and had a card Woody'd signed that said 'I ain't dead yet,' on it."[3]

That was not the last meeting between Guthrie and Dylan. The veteran and rookie songsters met several times and became good friends.

Back in Greenwich Village, the scrawny, young singer in his scruffy clothes stole any opportunity he could to play for an audience. He might do afternoons

*Woody Guthrie was Bob Dylan's idol. Late in Guthrie's life Dylan
befriended him while Guthrie was in a New Jersey state hospital.*

at the Café Wha?, then evening and night shows at similar clubs such as the Commons, the Limelight, and the Gaslight. On Sunday afternoons, he took his guitar and harmonica and sang for free in Washington Square Park. Between shows Dylan relaxed by playing chess with other up-and-coming folk singers or going to parties which often turned into huge, all-night jam sessions.

Weary of playing only other people's songs, Dylan tried his hand at writing his own. One of his first was a tribute to his hero titled simply, "Song to Woody." Others were humorous in nature, such as one inspired by a newspaper account of a family outing gone awry on an excursion boat on the Hudson River. Dylan titled it "Talking Bear Mountain Picnic Massacre Blues," and it always drew laughs from assembled crowds.

The nineteen-year-old Dylan gradually became known to area club owners and eventually got his first gig offering a real paycheck. It was at a place called Gerde's Folk City and Dylan debuted there on April 11, 1961. It was at Folk City that he met a pretty, dark-haired, seventeen-year-old fan named Suze (pronounced "Suzy") Rotolo. Before long, they were a couple and Suze happily followed Dylan around, sitting up front whenever he performed.

Suze and Bob appeared to be a great team. They were attracted to each other and were both dreamers. Years later Suze recalled, "We made a conscious effort of being by ourselves, shutting out the rest of the world."[4] In the nighttime, the couple hung around the coffeehouses and nightclubs of Greenwich Village.

*Guthrie dedicated himself to meeting and writing songs about good people who had fallen upon hard times during the Great Depression. Many of those Guthrie met lived out of tents or their own vehicles.*

By day, they spent time going to movies or visiting people, where they often spent afternoons together browsing through their friends' book collections. Then again, there were days when they would just relax and get lost in their thoughts while listening to music. And to top it off, Suze was a big fan of Woody Guthrie. She knew all of Guthrie's songs.

Things were progressing nicely for Bob Dylan. He spent the summer of 1961 making a name for himself. It was that fall when he made the acquaintance of John Hammond, impressed *The New York Times* music critic Robert Shelton, and inked his first recording contract.

But in the reality of the cutthroat business of the music world, Bob Dylan had a long way to go.

# Jammin' With Hammond's Folly

How does a newly signed musical artist get noticed? One way is for record companies to send information in the form of news releases about their performers to the media. Hopefully, a newspaper reporter or television broadcaster will then want to interview the person for a story. Of course, one with a fascinating background makes the best kind of story.

Dylan was aware of the power of publicity, and he also liked telling tall tales about himself. One of Dylan's earliest interviews was with Columbia Records's publicist Billy James in fall 1961. Dylan related to James a colorful history about his life, much of it false. He admitted he was from northern Minnesota but also claimed to have run away from home. How old was he at the time, James asked? "Uh, about seven. Seven—eight—something like that," Dylan answered.[1]

Dylan laid it on thicker and heavier as the interview continued. He claimed to have traveled the country working as a carnival roustabout, or unskilled laborer. Of his so-called carnival days, Dylan told James, "I didn't sing for any money but I learned a lot of songs in the carnival. Lots of songs that people are singing today I learned in that carnival. That's why I know all these songs they do now—at least a folk song—I've heard a version of it or something like it before."[2]

This fake Dylan biography was sent to much of the media, and people had no reason to believe it was not true.

Dylan recorded his first album for Columbia in November 1961. It included original numbers, such as "Song to Woody," but also his versions of standard blues and folk tunes such as "Pretty Peggy-O" and "House of the Risin' Sun." Then he had to wait for Columbia to release it to radio stations and record stores.

Early in 1962 Dylan hooked up with a manager, Albert Grossman. A manager's job is to take care of an entertainer's business affairs. Grossman would help Dylan decide how to negotiate contracts with Columbia Records, where it would be best to perform, and how to deal with the media. Based on Dylan's personality and talents, Grossman felt Dylan should appear aloof and mysterious. He should not talk frequently with reporters. When he did, he should not

*Dylan's first album was not a financial success but helped build a following of dedicated fans.*

say much. Instead of explaining what he meant in his lyrics, it would be best to allow his listeners to question them.

But Columbia Records was not in a rush to release Dylan's album. Even though Columbia paid Dylan to record it, there would be greater costs to press it and ship copies. Some Columbia executives wondered whether it was wise to invest any more money in the album. Many thought Dylan's voice was too strange for him to become successful. It was not rich like Elvis Presley's, or smooth like then teen idol Bobby Rydell.

In these early days of rock-and-roll, 45s carried much more weight than albums. The majority of radio stations played hit 45s, not album cuts. Albums were viewed as collections of an artist's hit singles, with a few throwaway songs included to fill space. Columbia's Director of Artists and Repertoire, Dave Kapralik, and other company executives felt there was not a single Dylan song on the album that had the potential to be a popular 45.

Kapralik and others thought John Hammond had made a big mistake in signing Dylan. Maybe Hammond had had success years ago with big band jazz, but this was a different music. The people who loved jazz greats such as Goodman, Basie, and Holiday were now in their mid-40s, and Kapralik felt Hammond was out of touch with the young people of the early 1960s. Those at Columbia referred to Dylan as "Hammond's Folly."

But Hammond was still sharp. He was convinced Dylan had what it took to be a smash and spoke to as many people as he could at Columbia, urging them to take a chance on this new talent. His efforts worked, and Dylan's first album was released on March 19, 1962. It was titled simply, *Bob Dylan*.

The album received some good reviews but was not a financial success. Kapralik said that was enough of a reason to drop Dylan's contract. Again, Hammond went to bat for Dylan. And again, he convinced Kapralik and other Columbia executives to keep him.

Dylan kept busy writing songs. One was a biting satire of an ultra-conservative political group called the John Birch Society. Dylan called it "Talkin' John Birch Paranoid Blues," and he used words like knives, brutally attacking the group as a bunch of closed-minded extremists.

Another new Dylan song was "Blowin' in the Wind." It is a haunting ballad in which Dylan asks questions about freedom, war, peace, and life, and death. But he does not give answers. He sings that the answers are "blowin' in the wind."

Many Dylan friends loved the song. They thought it was profound, and asked meaningful questions. Others were not sure. One respected folk singer named Dave Van Ronk first thought, "What an incredibly dumb song. I mean, what the hell is 'blowing in the wind?'"[3]

Abut a month and a half later, Van Ronk changed his mind. He recalled, "I was walking through Washington Square Park and heard a kid singing, 'How much wood could a woodchuck chuck if a woodchuck could chuck wood? The answer, my friend, is blowin' in the wind.'" At that point, I knew Bobby had a smash on his hands!"[4]

Dylan's relationship with his friend Suze Rotolo provided inspiration for another song. Bob and Suze had been having arguments in which she claimed that he was controlling her. Dylan responded that she did not appreciate him. He received no support from Suze's mother, Mary. To her, Dylan was an unwashed folk singer with a wise-guy attitude, and she treated him like he had a plague. Suze split up with Dylan, leading him to write a song called "Don't Think Twice, It's Alright." Unlike his songs with political themes, "Don't Think Twice, It's Alright" was about a scorned lover telling an ex-girlfriend good-bye and good riddance.

On August 9, 1962, Dylan officially said good-bye to Bobby Zimmerman and legally changed his name to Bob Dylan. He spent much of the following spring recording his second album. Outside the studio, he was setting off fireworks with his words and actions. He was rude to the media. In an interview for an alternative New York City newspaper, *The Village Voice*, Dylan was asked whether he was influenced by Hank Williams. Dylan responded, "Hey, look, I consider Hank Williams, Captain Marvel, Marlon Brando, The Tennessee Stud, Clark Kent, Walter Cronkite and J. Carroll Naish all influences. Now what is it— please—what is it exactly you people want to know?"[5]

Captain Marvel and Clark Kent are comic book characters. Walter Cronkite was a news anchor, The Tennessee Stud is a fictional horse, and J. Carroll

Naish was a character actor. Obviously, Dylan had no intention of taking the reporter's questions seriously.

Two months later, he made a decision which few up and coming entertainers would have the nerve to do. Dylan turned down a chance to appear on the May 12 *The Ed Sullivan Show*, one of the most-watched television programs in its day. It would have been wonderful publicity for his second album.

Dylan wanted to sing, "Talkin' John Birch Paranoid Blues." The show's staff would not allow him to perform it. They said it was too controversial and asked him if he would do something else. He quietly responded, "No, this is what I want to do. If I can't play my song, I'd rather not appear on the show."[6]

It turned out that not appearing on the Sullivan show may have been better for Dylan's career than actually performing. Young people heard about the incident and respected him for having the courage to stand up for what he believed in.

Dylan's second album, *The Freewheelin' Bob Dylan*, was released May 27, 1963. Featured on the cover was a photograph of Dylan walking side by side with Suze. The song that caused so much trouble, "Talkin' John Birch Paranoid Blues," was included on early copies but cut from later recordings. Dylan songs which did made the album included future classics "Blowin' in the Wind," and "Don't Think Twice, It's Alright." Almost all the album cuts were written by Dylan.

The album received rave reviews and was a major hit. It helped that a popular folk trio named Peter, Paul & Mary recorded "Blowin' in the Wind" and

*Ed Sullivan, host of one of the most popular TV shows in the 50's and 60's, invited Dylan to appear on his show. Dylan declined after learning he would not be allowed to sing a song that was considered too controversial. Sullivan is shown here, center, with The Beatles.*

released it as a 45 early in the summer. The trio had just had a huge hit with a 45 called "Puff (The Magic Dragon)." "Blowin' in the Wind" was a perfect follow-up song. It peaked at number 2 on the national chart that summer. Peter, Paul & Mary followed up that hit with Dylan's "Don't Think Twice, It's Alright," which made it to number 9.[7]

"Blowin' in the Wind" was the stand-out song from Dylan's second album. It represented the ideas and dreams of liberal young people who wanted to make a difference in the world. Dylan sang it in late July at his first appearance at the Newport Folk Festival, an annual event in Newport, Rhode Island, showcasing the best folk performers in the world. Critics said Dylan was the hit of the show. In just a few months, Dylan had grown from just another singer with talent to a folk music superstar.

Suze and Bob decided to get back together that year. Meanwhile, Dylan continued to work on new songs and do live concerts for the rest of 1963. In August, he performed at the famous March on Washington, where Dr. Martin Luther King, Jr., gave his historic "I Have a Dream" speech.

Then on October 26, he played in a place reserved for only the world's most respected musicians: Carnegie Hall in New York City. Dylan flew his parents in from Minnesota for the show. They were delighted to see their son play but some reporters said he was rude to them afterwards by ignoring them after his performance.

With Dylan now famous, the press started researching his past. Many establishment reporters were thrilled to tell their readers that Bob Dylan was as phony as a three-dollar bill. In its November 4, 1963, issue, *Newsweek* magazine quoted Dylan saying, "I don't know my parents. They don't know me. I've lost contact with them for years."[8] In the following sentence, *Newsweek* said, "A few blocks away Mr. and Mrs. Abe Zimmerman of Hibbing, Minn. were looking forward to seeing their son sing at Carnegie Hall. Bobby had paid their way east and had sent them tickets."[9]

What a liar, *Newsweek* readers must have thought. People who did not like his style reveled in the report. But his fans did not seem to mind. That included perhaps his biggest fan at the time, a well-known folk singer named Joan Baez. She had warmly introduced Dylan at Newport, and soon they were seeing each other romantically. Dylan was still seeing Suze as well. Dylan historians have differing views on how much Suze and Joan knew about each other at that time.

Dylan's third album *The Times They are A-Changin'* came out in February 1964. The title song became its best known cut. It was a ballad which called on young people to stand up to racism and unjustness. He also directly attacked bigotry with a song called, "The Lonesome Death of Hattie Carroll.' It was based on a true story of a wealthy white man who murdered an African-American waitress and served a mere six months in prison as punishment. However, not everything on the album involved social issues. It also included a melancholy love song titled "One

Too Many Mornings," thought to be about Dylan's relationship with Suze Rotolo.

Dylan's newfound fame was having an effect on him. On one hand, he enjoyed the attention, but only when he was in the right mood. On the other hand, he was annoyed by his sudden lack of privacy. People approached him on the street to ask for autographs and discuss political issues. Others claimed to be old friends and requested special favors. Dylan decided he needed a break.

A couple of days after the release of *The Times They Are A-Changin'*, Dylan and three friends took off on a lengthy road trip. They did not plan to stop at tourist attractions but to meet the real people of America, as Woody Guthrie had. First, they brought clothes to striking coal miners in Kentucky. They then paused in New Orleans, where Dylan encountered racial segregation firsthand. Dylan found it disturbing when an African-American man they had befriended was not allowed to enter a restaurant with them.

On New Orleans's famed Bourbon Street, they joined a crowd surrounding a street musician playing "Don't Think Twice, It's Alright." Dylan told the kid he played well. When he started singing along to the man's next tune, the singer stopped suddenly, spurting out, "You! I mean. It couldn't be. No, it's impossible!" Dylan simply replied, "You sing that very well," and moved on.[10]

The road trip ended in California where Dylan appeared on a television show and met up with Joan Baez. When Dylan returned to New York in March, Suze Rotolo confronted him. Again, she accused

*Bob Dylan and singer Joan Baez were romantically involved until they split in 1964. This photograph shows them at the Civil Rights March on Washington, D.C., on August 28, 1963.*

Dylan of controlling her. She also suspected that he and Joan Baez had gotten together in California. Dylan and Rotolo split for good.

Rotolo later said, "As Dylan got more and more famous, things got more and more oppressive. It was a whole bad time and I really crumbled. I didn't see myself as Bob Dylan's wife. All I wanted to do was get away from it all."[11]

Though finished with Suze, Dylan continued dating Joan Baez. But he also started seeing a different woman he had met several months earlier. She was an exotic, dark-haired beauty named Sara Lowndes. Sara, a friend of Albert Grossman's wife, was a twenty-five-year-old divorced woman with a young daughter named Maria.

# My Hands
# Are on Fire

Something wild was happening on the music scene while Dylan was traveling cross-country. The British group The Beatles had taken over the world of music like a rocket. Through the winter and spring of 1964, one Beatles song after another hit number one on the American charts. Some had been recorded as many as two years earlier and had already been hits in Europe. It had taken a while for the group consisting of John Lennon, Paul McCartney, George Harrison, and Ringo Starr to catch on in the United States. But once they did, American musical tastes would never be the same.

Rock songs replaced acoustic folk music in popularity. It seemed that almost any British musical group could bang out a record and get airplay in the

United States. This list included not just the Beatles, but the Rolling Stones, The Dave Clark Five, the Kinks, the Animals, and Gerry and the Pacemakers. People in the music business called this "the British invasion."

The sudden change in music was absolutely shocking. Some of the most established hit-makers, such as Connie Francis, the Shirelles, Chubby Checker, and the Everly Brothers saw their careers suddenly stop dead in their tracks.

How did this affect Bob Dylan? At first, not much. He still had his usual folk fanatics who tried to figure out hidden meanings in his songs and anxiously awaited every new Dylan album. At the Newport Folk

*Dylan was a popular signer at the Newport Folk Festival. Shown here is folk singer Jim Kweskin at a Newport Folk Festival workshop.*

Festival in July 1964, he debuted two new songs, "All I Really Want to Do" and "It Ain't Me, Babe." Both were personal numbers about friendship and love, and some in the audience were disappointed that he shied away from political material. That assignment was left to Dylan's girlfriend Joan Baez, who closed the Friday evening concert with the unofficial anthem of the civil rights movement, "We Shall Overcome."

Dylan's next album, *Another Side of Bob Dylan*, came out in August 1964 and included the two songs he premiered a month earlier in Newport. Dylan insisted the album's title was his producer's idea. Dylan later said, "I didn't want them to call [my fourth album] Another Side of Bob Dylan because I thought it was just too corny."[1]

It was not a colorful title, but it did make fans wonder, "What other side?" One Dylan historian explained, "The 'another side' it showed was his inside."[2] That meant that the songs were more about Dylan's feelings rather than social issues. Many critics panned the album, saying it did not have the creativity of his earlier work. Fans bought copies, but not as many as they had of his previous two albums.

While Dylan had recorded four albums and had become a household name across the world, he was just twenty-three years old. Most people at that age are recent college graduates just starting out in their careers. Like many people that young, Dylan was busy experimenting with his life. About this time he began taking LSD, an illegal chemical compound that causes people to hallucinate, or see and perceive things that are not there. Marijuana had been part of the folk scene for some time. But LSD is a much more dangerous drug. As the 1960s progressed, drug use among musicians and other young people would spread.

Dylan's next album, *Bringing It All Back Home,* was released in March 1965. It included both rock-influenced songs and traditional acoustic numbers. One, "Subterranean Homesick Blues," would become a Dylan classic. "Subterranean Homesick Blues" was a long way from the simple questions of "Blowin' in the Wind." It was a fast-paced number full of rapid-fire lyrics of basic rhymes, taking on everything from the education system to the government.

Considering how popular Dylan was, it was amazing that he had never had a hit 45. "Subterranean Homesick Blues" was his first. It peaked at number 39 in May.[3]

Around the same time that *Bringing It All Back Home* came out, Dylan made a brief side trip into movies. A filmmaker named Donn Pennebaker shot a documentary film of a Dylan tour in England in the spring of 1965. It was called *Don't Look Back* and was shot in a technique called cinema verite. There was no script. Pennebaker shot action as it happened, whether it was Dylan singing in concert or arguing with a reporter from *Time* magazine. It played in big city theaters specializing in art films. Critics were divided in their opinions. Those who liked Dylan also liked the movie. Those who were not Dylan fans blasted it. One newspaper, *The Atlanta Journal,* called it a "boring, off-color home movie of the neighborhood's biggest brat blowing his nose for 90 minutes."[4]

Of course, newspapers were never among Dylan's biggest supporters, since he continued to toy with reporters. He said to a member of the British press that year, "Actually, the first record I made was in 1935."[5] That would have been an amazing trick considering that Dylan was born in 1941.

Dylan and Sara Lowndes were becoming closer as a couple. It seemed that the more he saw of Sara, the less he respected Joan Baez. Baez wrote a letter to her sister Mimi while on tour with Dylan in May 1964. In it she said, "We're leaving Bobby's entourage. He has become so unbelievably unmanageable that I can't stand to be around him."[6]

Dylan's sixth album, *Highway 61 Revisited*, was released in August. It included "Like a Rolling Stone," which had been released as a 45 and peaked at number 2 that summer. Many critics have said "Like a Rolling Stone" is Dylan's best ever song. It is a rambling tune, lasting about six minutes. On the surface, it seems mean-spirited. Dylan appears to be getting pleasure from the troubles of an old girlfriend who once acted as if she was better than he. But like much of Dylan's words, those to "Like a Rolling Stone" can be taken on different levels. Music critic Robert Shelton says the song is "about the loss of innocence and the harshness of experience."[7]

"Like a Rolling Stone" makes prominent use of guitar, harmonica, Dylan's straining voice, and the intense organ work of keyboard player Al Kooper. It was very different from Dylan's early songs in which he accompanied himself only by acoustic guitar.

This was part of the new trend. Not all folk

diehards accepted it, as proven by a very controversial appearance he made at the 1965 Newport Folk Festival.

Over the years, Dylan's performance on that July day on the Rhode Island coast has become a folk tale in itself. What really happened has never been clear. Even those in attendance have not agreed on what took place.

The most-told story of July 25, 1965, goes like this: Dylan came onstage sporting not his usual acoustic guitar, but an electric one and with a rock band behind him. He played three songs. The first was a pro-labor tune he wrote called "Maggie's Farm." A chorus of boos was heard from the audience.

Dylan's second and third songs were "Like A Rolling Stone" and "It Takes a Lot to Laugh, It Takes a Train to Cry." The booing did not let up. In response, Dylan left the stage. He returned with an acoustic guitar and played two folk songs in the traditional manner. The audience then accepted him, after giving him a clear message that they would not allow him to ruin folk music by cheapening it.

But what really happened? A music historian named Sam Charters studied films and recordings of Dylan's short electric set and insisted the only loud objections from audience members were about the quality of the sound system. Charters said, "There were no boos and the complaints weren't about the music—My God, Dylan was the hottest thing going. The sound system at Newport was not set up properly for electric instruments, so people were yelling out because all they could hear was noise."[8]

Dylan's organ player Al Kooper said years later

that the audience booed because Dylan's music set was too short. He griped, "We've read the untrue accounts for so many years."[9] The person at the sound console, Paul Rothchild, was in charge of controlling the loudness of Dylan's music. He recalled things a bit differently. "From my perspective, it seemed like everybody on my left wanted Dylan to get off the stage, everybody on my right wanted him to turn it up. And I did—I turned it up."[10]

Dylan was convinced the audience was booing him personally. According to Dylan, "They certainly booed, I'll tell you that. You could hear it all over the place. I was kind of stunned. But I can't put anybody down for coming and booing. After all, they paid to get in. They could have been maybe a little quieter and not so persistent, though."[11]

When Dylan came back onstage with his acoustic guitar, he sang one of his own compositions, "It's All Over Now, Baby Blue." Was he telling the audience that his period as a folk purist was all over?

According to Paul Rothchild, "To me, that night at Newport was as clear as crystal. It's the end of one era and the beginning of another."[12]

Later that night, several Newport musicians had a get-together. Dylan sat alone, depressed. A singer named Maria Muldaur thought he might cheer up if she asked him to dance. The saddened Dylan replied with an odd response: "I would dance with you, Maria, but my hands are on fire."[13] The entire episode was one of many curious incidents in the strange and eventful life of Bob Dylan.

Despite the fact that Dylan was now writing songs

with personal as well as social messages, college students continued to hold him in high regard. In an informal survey taken at three Ivy League colleges that fall, students voted Dylan their "favorite contemporary American writer."[14]

Not all students felt that way. One said "it was 'absurd' to take Dylan's writing seriously."[15]

But enough respected his words that several music artists around this time jumped on the Dylan bandwagon. They recorded Dylan songs which in turn became hit 45s. A Los Angeles band, the Byrds, had a number-one smash with an electrified version of "Mr. Tambourine Man."[16] Another band from Los Angeles, the Turtles, took their version of "It Ain't Me Babe" to number 8 in the fall of 1965.[17] Current superstar Cher had her first solo hit with Dylan's song "All I Really Want To Do." It reached number 15 that same fall.[18] A few months later, one of rock music's finest vocal groups, the Four Seasons, recorded an up-tempo version of "Don't Think Twice" under the fake name, The Wonder Who. It peaked at number 12.[19]

In homes across America, teenagers tuned their radios to local rock stations, just as young Bobby Zimmerman had in his Minnesota home ten years earlier. Instead of hearing the music of Little Richard as Dylan had, they were tuned into the songs of Dylan himself. It did not matter if they were sung by Dylan or some other group. Dylan had become a full-fledged star. The question on the minds of rock fans was, "What would Bob Dylan do next?"

# 7

# Cheating Death

Dylan spent the fall of 1965 touring eastern cities with his electric guitar and backup band. As at Newport, some fans would boo and yell at him to get off the stage. At a concert at the Forest Hills Music center in New York City, people yelled out, "We want the old Dylan."[1] *The New York Times* music critic Robert Shelton called the audience "rude and immature," and wrote, "By the time they [the audience] get to know his excellent new folk rock songs, maybe the noisy young boors who ruined an artistically strong concert may have grown up a bit."[2]

But Dylan's rock-oriented fans loved Dylan's new sound and celebrated it by dancing in the aisles. Between the battle of the folkies and the rockers, the rockers were winning.

Dylan took time off from touring to marry Sara Lowndes in the Long Island town of Mineola, New York, on November 22, 1965. The ceremony was small and so secret that he did not even tell his parents, brother, or best friends. Why Dylan remained so silent about his marriage is unknown, but it is believed that he just wanted privacy. The last thing he wanted was for the media to butt into his personal life. Just about two months after the marriage, Sara gave birth to a son, Jesse Byron Dylan, on January 6, 1966. The public learned about the baby when a newspaper, *The New York Post*, discovered and reported it on February 9, 1966.

The question, "What would Bob Dylan do next?" was answered in May 1966, when his album titled, *Blonde on Blonde* was released. It is to many Dylan critics his all-time finest album. It was also his first not recorded in New York. Dylan's then-producer Bob Johnston suggested recording the record in Nashville, Tennessee, the city known as the capital of country music. Johnston knew several Nashville musicians who could play backup. It also helped that Dylan's record label, Columbia, has a superb recording facility in Nashville.

*Blonde on Blonde* contained songs which have become Dylan classics. A ballad, "Just Like a Woman," was about male and female relationships. Some have criticized it for being demeaning to women but like many Dylan songs, different people have various interpretations. Other often-played cuts from *Blonde on Blonde* include the mournful "Stuck Inside Mobile with the Memphis Blue Again," and "I Want

You," in which he pleads for a woman not to leave him.

But the most controversial and successful number was a rolling, raucous party song with a loud horn section. Its title was "Rainy Day Women #12 and 35."

The words in the title appear nowhere in the song. The frequently repeated chorus goes, "Everybody must get stoned." The word stoned once meant being drunk. With widespread drug-use among young people in the 1960s, the meaning changed to being high on marijuana. Those who took the song at face-value believed it was a drug song, and that a "rainy day woman" was slang for a marijuana cigarette.

The song was released as a 45 and reached number two on the national chart early in the summer of 1966.[3] That was in spite of the fact that many radio stations refused to play it.

Was the song really about drugs? Some said Dylan's use of the word "stoned" was meant to be taken literally. Stoning somebody, or hitting them with stones until they die, is a common punishment in the Bible. Dylan could have been saying that any person who takes a stand will be "stoned." That did not mean he or she would be put to death, but be snubbed or shut out by others. When asked, Dylan simply answered that he never would write a song about drugs.

True or not, Dylan's friends noticed in the mid-1960s that Dylan was heavily using drugs. His skin had turned pale and his eyes drooped. Dylan appeared nervous and shaky. Friends said he would stay up for days without sleeping. He was not only rude to the media, but to those who knew him.

These problems did not stop Dylan from going on a world concert tour. One night in Stockholm, Sweden, Dylan and his crew were walking by the docks of the port city when they saw an American Navy destroyer anchored there.

At this time the Vietnam War was raging and dividing the American public. Rock musicians, including Dylan, and others were questioning whether the United States was right to be involved in the war. On the other side were the military and their supporters who felt it was unpatriotic to disagree with America's support of South Vietnam against communist North Vietnam. It was a heated issue and became the basis for emotional arguments in both classrooms and living rooms across the country. In addition, many rock musicians, with their grubby clothes and long hair, contrasted greatly with the clean-cut looks and spit-and-polish uniforms of the military.

Dylan's crew wanted to leave the wharf area for fear some Navy men would try to start a fight with them. Just as they feared, the ship's first officer exited the destroyer and approached the star. "Are you Bob Dylan," the officer asked. "Yeah, I'm Bob Dylan. What's it to you?" the singer answered.

The captain answered, "I just want to tell you that I wrote a novel called *One Too Many Mornings*. Your song was the most incredible thing I ever heard. It changed my life, and I wanted to thank you myself."[4] He shook Dylan's hand and returned to the ship. The singer turned and smiled to his crew like the Cheshire Cat from *Alice in Wonderland.*

But Dylan's drug addiction was apparent on the tour. He often slurred words while on stage. While riding in a limousine with John Lennon of the Beatles one night, Dylan was so ill he vomited in the back seat. Dylan returned to New York in June, sick and exhausted. He learned that his manager Albert Grossman had booked him for sixty more concerts. In need of a break, Dylan went to the town of Woodstock, New York where he kept a retreat. Woodstock is a country town about one hundred miles from New York City at the base of the Catskill Mountains. Artists and writers are attracted to its beauty and small town features, and Dylan was right at home.

In late July Dylan cheated death again. And once more, it had to do with a motorcycle. Dylan told his friend and music critic Robert Shelton that after being awake for three days, he was taking his bike to a repair shop. On the way, he hit an oil slick. The back-wheel locked and Dylan was thrown over the handlebars. However, that is only one of many stories about what happened. Another account says that he was simply doing wheelies at his home and he took the spill. Regardless, it began a major change in Dylan's life.

Dylan recovered from his injuries, then for the next few years practically quit show business. He also dropped out from public sight. He reduced—and according to some people, ended—his dependency on drugs, and enjoyed spending time with his family, which was growing. A daughter, Anna, was born on

July 11, 1967 followed by a son named Samuel on July 30, 1968 and another son, Jakob, on December 9, 1969.

Why did Dylan take the time off from his career? A few years later, he said, "I didn't sense the importance of that accident till at least a year after [it happened.] I realized that it was a real accident. I mean I thought that I was just gonna get up and go back to doing what I was doing before, but I couldn't do it anymore."[5]

Even though he quit making public appearances, Dylan did not stop writing and recording. He jammed with five back-up musicians who later became a successful rock group called The Band. They played Dylan compositions, as well as folk standards in both a room in Dylan's home and in the basement of a house his back-up musicians rented and nicknamed Big Pink. Once in a while they taped their music, but Dylan had no immediate intention of releasing these sessions on albums.

On the other hand, he did record albums meant to be released. One, titled *John Wesley Harding*, came out in January 1968. Except for a greatest hits collection which came out in the spring of 1967, it was his first album since *Blonde on Blonde*. The album was named for a real Wild West figure named John Wesley Hardin who shot and killed a sheriff. While in prison, Hardin studied law and was released early. He began to practice his new trade in El Paso, Texas, but just a year later he was killed by a law officer.

With the Vietnam War more divisive than ever, a new kind of hero began to emerge among young people:

the anti-hero. These were people who did good but rebelled against authority or sometimes broke the law to do so. Many who felt the Vietnam War was immoral burned their draft cards in public and refused to be inducted into the armed service. They were anti-heroes—those who broke the law to do what they thought was right. In a similar manner, John Wesley Hardin was an anti-hero.

Dylan's hero, Woody Guthrie, died in 1967 and several musicians planned a memorial concert. Dylan came out of his retreat to perform three songs with the Band. The next year he released another album, *Nashville Skyline*, which received mixed reviews but sold well. He also appeared at a huge music festival on the Isle of Wight, in Great Britain. Curiously, he did not appear at perhaps the most famous rock concert of all time, the original Woodstock, which took place not far from his home. The storied 1969 three-day concert featured headline bands and drew hundreds of thousands of fans.

Of all the possible locations for such a noteworthy rock concert, why was the Woodstock, New York, area, chosen? A newspaper writer named Al Aronowitz said, "In essence, the Woodstock Festival was nothing but a call to Bob to come out and play."[6]

Dylan later stated that he ignored Woodstock because he was sick of uninvited fans coming to his house day and night. "They kept comin'. This was just about the time of that Woodstock festival, which was the sum total of all this. I couldn't get any space for myself and my family, and there was no help, nowhere.

I got very resentful about the whole thing, and we got outta there."[7]

The next year, 1970, he released two more albums. One, *Self Portrait*, was a two-record set and was disliked by most critics and fans. The next, *New Morning*, was better received. In September, Dylan left his country home and moved back to Greenwich Village in New York City. With many singers and celebrities there, Dylan would not stand out as he did in small Woodstock.

Dylan turned thirty in 1971 and celebrated his birthday quietly in Tel Aviv, Israel, with his family. He appeared to be getting in touch with his religion, which he had mostly ignored since his childhood. Dylan prayed at the Western Wall, the only remaining

*Woodstock would prove to be the most famous rock concert of the 1960s.*

remnant of the second temple in Jerusalem and dating to the year 70 A.D. It is the holiest site in Judaism. Dylan said, "I'm a Jew. It touches my poetry, my life, in ways I can't describe."[8]

He released two 45s in 1971, but other than a second greatest hits collection, no new album. In August, he appeared at a benefit concert in New York City to aid poverty-stricken refugees in Bangladesh, a war-ravaged country once a province of Pakistan. Then in November, he purchased property for a new home a bit north of the wealthy seaside community of Malibu, in southern California. Much of the recording industry had relocated from New York to California, so Dylan decided he should make the move, too.

And it was closer to Mexico where Dylan was on his way in November 1972 to do something new—film a major Hollywood movie.

# Catching the Eye of the Hurricane

$M$any renowned singers made a successful leap from music to movies. These included Frank Sinatra, the Beatles, and Elvis Presley. Now it was Bob Dylan's turn to try his hand at acting.

Movie director Sam Peckinpah was a hard-living, temperamental man known for violence in his films. The movie he tapped Dylan for was a western titled *Pat Garrett and Billy the Kid*. It was based on a true story of two outlaws who were friends in the Old West. Billy the Kid, whose real name was William Bonney, murdered twenty-one men and lacked respect for human life. Pat Garrett became a sheriff and was ordered to find and capture his old friend Billy, dead or alive.

The movie was not a simple action story. It had numerous themes including friendship, loyalty, and lawlessness. The title characters were treated as anti-heroes. Dylan played a man named Alias, a printer's assistant who becomes one of Billy the Kid's followers.

Filming began in Durango, Mexico, on November 13, 1972, and lasted roughly four months. Reporters came from all over to write articles about Bob Dylan's new endeavor. Even though Dylan's part was small, he received more attention than the lead actors. Typically, Dylan refused to talk to the media, who had to speak with people working with him to get their stories.

The movie was released the next summer to mixed reviews. Some said it was slow moving while others felt it was a strong character study. Dylan also composed the movie soundtrack, which was released as an album and reached number 12 on the national album chart.[1] One cut, a haunting ballad titled "Knockin' on Heaven's Door," was released as a 45 and went to number 12.[2]

Although the soundtrack was a hit with the public, several music critics hated it. Vincent Canby of the important *The New York Times* wrote, "The music is so oppressive that when it stops we feel giddy with relief, as if a tooth had suddenly stopped aching."[3]

With his debut acting job behind him, Dylan embarked on his first tour since the motorcycle accident. He played forty huge shows from early January through mid-February 1973. Members of The Band and others played backup. A total of 658,000 combined tickets were offered for all the concerts, and every one was sold.[4] Fans screamed their approval as Dylan did both acoustic and electric sets.

Dylan's next album, released the same time the tour was taking place, was called *Planet Waves* and became Dylan's first to reach number one on the national album chart.[5] *Planet Waves* was followed by two more hit albums, 1974's *Before the Flood*, which hit number 3, and *Blood on the Tracks*, which also made number one.[6] There was no mistake about it: Bob Dylan was back.

Things were going well in the mid-1970s. Bob and Sara got busy building a mansion on their California property, and Dylan also bought a farm near Minneapolis, Minnesota, to use as a retreat. He was less angry with the press but still avoided dealing with them whenever possible. Dylan also began to play up the importance of religion in his life. In an interview he said, "I don't care what people expect of me. Doesn't concern me. I'm doin' God's work. That's all I know."[7] In another one, he was asked how he imagines God. Dylan declared, "I can see God in a daisy. I can see God at night in the wind and rain. I see creation just about everywhere."[8]

Anything with Dylan's name on it seemed to turn to gold. The tapes Dylan had privately made with the Band in Woodstock in 1967 had been released illegally over the last several years. Illegal recordings are called bootlegs. They become available when someone obtains copies of the original recordings and makes and sells their own copies. It is against the law since the recording artist receives nothing for his or her work. Dylan and Columbia Records decided they might as well make an official recording of those tapes.

A total of twenty-four songs from the sessions were released in July 1975 on a two-album set titled *The Basement Tapes*. Critics raved, calling it one of Dylan's best. While it did not sell as well as Dylan's newest material, *The Basement Tapes* was a hit nonetheless, reaching number 7 on the national album chart.[9]

Although *Planet Waves* and *Blood on the Tracks* were heavy with personal songs about relationships, Dylan did not give up political activism. An advertising executive named George Lois had gotten wind of a true story of what appeared to be an example of failed justice. Professional middle-weight boxer Rubin "Hurricane" Carter and a man named John Artis were convicted of murdering three white men in a Paterson, New Jersey, bar in 1966.

Carter and Artis, both African Americans, insisted they were innocent. They claimed they had been framed by dishonest white police officers and a racist court system. Two men who identified Carter and Artis in court were Arthur Dexter Bradley and Alfred Bello, who were committing a burglary near the scene of the shootings. Then in 1974, both Bradley and Bello admitted lying under oath. The case was officially reopened and Carter and Artis were given new trials.

Carter was no angel. He had a strong temper and had been convicted of crimes such as petty theft. In a 1964 magazine, Carter was quoted as saying white police officers should be killed. He later explained that his words had been taken out of context.

Still, George Lois believed Carter did not commit murder and began championing the fighter's cause. Lois sent a copy of Carter's autobiography, *The Sixteenth Round*, to celebrities including Dylan. Dylan was so touched by the book that he visited Carter in prison. Convinced that Carter had been framed, Dylan and a co-writer named Jacques Levy composed a song telling Carter's version of the case. The song, "Hurricane," appeared on Dylan's next album, *Desire*, and was also released as a 45. It made the top forty, but was often played on FM stations, which at the time generally did not play pop 45s. George Lois played a tape of the song to Carter while visiting him in prison. Lois recalled, "He lost his mind! It was beautiful. There was (sic) tears in his eyes. He was crying."[10]

Meanwhile, Dylan busily organized his next tour. It would be something new—a sort of cross between a rock concert and alternative theater. Dylan called it the Rolling Thunder Revue.

Dylan would play small-town theaters and auditoriums as well as massive arenas. While Dylan would have regular back-up musicians, the tour was open to well-known entertainers who felt like dropping by to share the stage. These included his old friend Joan Baez; folk star Joni Mitchell; African-American ballad singer Roberta Flack; Canadian guitarist and folk-pop singer Gordon Lightfoot; and Arlo Guthrie, son of Dylan's hero Woody Guthrie and a successful singer in his own right. Some guest stars did not sing; poet

Allen Ginsberg recited his works on stage. At one stop in Toronto, even Dylan's mother Beatty made an appearance.

Dylan usually went onstage wearing a fedora hat, faded jeans, and a black vest over a white shirt. Some nights his face was painted white. Critics and fans analyzed what kind of statement he was trying to make by appearing in whiteface. Was he making a comment on some kind of injustice in society? Dylan gave what some said to be a misleading answer: He just wanted people in the back rows to be able to see his face. A performer with the Rolling Thunder Revue, singer and actress Ronee Blakley, summed up the tour's electric atmosphere. "It was like the circus came to town," she announced.[11]

Two concerts, in New York City and Houston, were designated as benefits to help pay for a new trial for Hurricane Carter, now out on bail. At the New York concert, celebrated heavy-weight boxing champ Muhammad Ali pleaded with the audience to get involved in Carter's cause. In March, Carter's and Artis's convictions were thrown out by a New Jersey court that ruled that they did not get a fair trial.

To top things off, Dylan decided to have the concert tour taped. He wanted to make a movie including tour scenes. It would be somewhat different from his earlier concert tour movie, *Don't Look Back.* This would have concert scenes but also include rehearsed dialogue and a plot. Dylan's wife Sara would have a starring role in this film to be called *Renaldo and Clara.*

*Famed boxer Muhammed Ali and Dylan supported a new trial for Hurricane Carter who had been convicted of shooting a police officer. Ali is pictured here with President Jimmy Carter.*

Who were Renaldo and Clara? True to type, Dylan answered evasively.

To one reporter he announced, "Renaldo is a fox and Clara is supposedly the clear understanding of the future which doesn't exist."[12] Who could even figure out what that meant?

About this time Bob and Sara Dylan's marriage was starting to fall apart. They argued about all sorts of things ranging from Dylan's rock-and-roll lifestyle to how their California mansion should be designed. There were rumors that Dylan was having extramarital relationships with women in his show, and that he had returned to smoking and drug use.

Dylan was part of one other concert film in 1976. The Band was splitting up and arranged a farewell show in San Francisco. As a tribute to his friends, Dylan announced he would join them for four songs. Since he did not want this concert movie to compete with *Renaldo and Clara*, Dylan allowed director Martin Scorsese to film him singing only two songs. The film was titled *The Last Waltz*, and is regarded by numerous critics as one of the best concert films ever made.

In late fall, Hurricane Carter was again put on trial. The happiness of Dylan and other Carter supporters turned to dismay as Bello and Bradley changed their stories once more and said they told the full truth in the first trial. Carter and Artis were found guilty again in December 1976 and resentenced to life in prison.

Meanwhile, on March 1, 1977, Sara Dylan filed for divorce. A court gave Sara custody of the children, and she moved the family from Malibu to Beverly Hills where the children attended school.

The praise afforded to *The Last Waltz* was not given to *Renaldo and Clara*. Dylan's movie premiered in New York and Los Angeles on January 25, 1978. Nearly every critic hated it. For one thing, the movie was nearly four hours long. Some felt it was hard to follow. *The New York Times* gave it one of its better reviews, though it was not a glowing one. It said, "The film contains more than its share of dead weight, but it is seldom genuinely dull."[13]

Dylan had spent $1.25 million of his own money making *Renaldo and Clara*. It earned very little in return.[14] Meanwhile, he had many bills to pay for both the construction of his mansion and the lawyers handling his divorce. To earn money, he embarked on a lengthy world tour in February 1978, which took him to four continents.

While on tour, he had a romantic relationship with an African-American back-up singer named Helena Springs. He soon began seeing Mary Alice Artes and Carolyn Dennis, other African-American women. All three had strong links to Christianity. A very controversial period of Dylan's life was about to begin.

# Time for Me to Do Something Else

Mary Alice Artes was active in an evangelical church called the Vineyard Fellowship. Evangelical Christians believe strongly that the Bible is the word of God and that the only way to heaven is accepting Jesus as one's savior. They generally are very conservative politically, believing the opposite of the views Dylan had always strongly supported.

Artes introduced Dylan to the ministers at her church and Dylan was taken with them. Before long he was regularly attending Bible classes and services at the Vineyard Fellowship. Dylan was soon baptized and officially admitted into the Christian faith.

Dylan said that although Artes had led him to the fellowship, it was a personal and mystical experience with Jesus that made him a Christian. He recalled a morning in his Malibu house when he stated, "There was a presence in the room that couldn't have been anybody but Jesus. I truly had a born-again experience, if you want to call it that. It was a physical thing. I felt it all over me. I felt my whole body tremble."[1]

Early in 1979, Dylan began recording a new album titled *Slow Train Coming*, with songs reflective of his newfound Christian faith. A single from the album, "Gotta Serve Somebody," became a top forty hit, reaching number 24 in the fall of 1979.[2] The album was even bigger, reaching number 3 on the national album chart.[3]

Christianity took over Dylan's life. When he went on tour to promote his new album, he and his musicians prayed before each performance. One night he did not think he would be able to sing since he had a sore throat. His singers prayed for him before the show. Dylan seemed to recover and did his show as usual.

Even though *Slow Train Coming* sold well, not all accepted the new religious Bob Dylan. The majority of his longtime fans could not stand to hear Dylan preaching through his music. He was booed at nearly every concert he played that year.

Dylan's family and Jewish friends found the legendary singer's Christianity insulting. They felt he had become a traitor to his faith. Dylan said he had expected angry reactions. "Not surprised at all," he answered when asked about them. He played up the minority who accepted his new music. "I'm just surprised to hear applause every time I play. I appreciate that. You can feel everything that comes off an audience.

Princeton University Library

*Bob Dylan receives an honorary degree from Princeton University in 1970. Dylan wrote his song "Day of the Locusts" based on the event.*

. . . little individual things that are going on. It's a very instant thing."[4]

In February 1980, Dylan won his first Grammy award. The Grammys are given by members of the recording industry for excellence in music. For decades, music critics faulted the Grammys for ignoring rock and roll while rewarding mostly middle-of-the-road music. Now, they were finally recognizing rock music with its own categories. Dylan won his award for his 45 "Gotta Serve Somebody," in the category of "Best Male Rock Vocal Performance."

His next album, *Saved*, released in June 1980, included more original songs about Christian beliefs. It did not sell nearly as well as *Slow Train Coming*, reaching 24 on the national album chart. While *Slow Train Coming* stayed on the chart twenty-six weeks, *Saved* lasted only eleven. It was his worst charting album since *Another Side of Bob Dylan* in 1964.[5]

Some fans and critics did not believe Dylan was a true Christian. They theorized that he felt empty and depressed following his divorce and grabbed on to the first new idea he came across. Others said he turned to Christianity only to please his girlfriend. Still others insisted Dylan was recording Christian music only to make money. The Born-Again Christian movement was growing in the United States. The United States President, Jimmy Carter, was a born-again Christian. Keith Richards of the Rolling Stones said Dylan was merely a "prophet of profit."[6]

Despite such talk, Dylan seemed sincere. He stated publicly, "What Jesus does for an ignorant man like myself is to make the qualities and characteristics of God more believable to me, cos I can't beat the devil. Only God can."[7]

Regardless of his newfound faith, the next several months were troubling ones. A fan named Carmel Hubbell became obsessed with Dylan. She insisted she had once been Dylan's girlfriend and began referring to herself as Carmel Dylan. Hubbell constantly phoned Dylan and his staff and followed him to theaters where he performed.

Then on December 8, 1980, a tragic event occurred when a crazed fan named Mark David Chapman shot and killed John Lennon of the Beatles. Dylan panicked that there would be copy-cat attacks on other musicians. He sent security people in advance to check the concert halls where he was to play and went so far as to buy one of his back-up musicians a bullet-proof vest.[8]

With fear for his safety in the back of his mind, Dylan tried to carry on. Carmel Hubbell did not make it easy. In June 1981, she barged into the studio where he was recording, only to be forced out by Dylan's staff. She then moved into an apartment close to Dylan's California home and began leaving threatening notes. At Dylan's urging, a court served Hubbell a restraining order, forcing her by law to stay away from the singer.

Dylan's third and last Christian-themed album, *Shot of Love*, came out in September 1981. It was a bit of a departure from *Slow Train Coming* and *Saved* in that it included non-religious songs. Like *Saved*, it did not sell well, reaching number 33 on the national album chart, and staying for a measly nine weeks.[9] But with secular songs on the album, it appeared Dylan was going back to his old form.

Early in 1982, there was another nightmare in Dylan's life. One of his best friends, Howard Alk, died of a drug overdose. Between the deaths of Alk and John Lennon, the threats from Carmel Hubbell, the rejection of many of his true fans, and a lawsuit filed by his manager, Albert Grossman, Dylan had had enough. As he did after his motorcycle accident in 1966, Dylan took a break from performing in public.

Those who followed Dylan's life noted that he seemed to be returning to his Jewish roots. In 1982, he celebrated his son Samuel's bar mitzvah. Then in the fall of 1983, Dylan's son Jesse had his bar

*Dylan is shown on left at the bar-mitzvah of his son Jesse (on right) at the Western Wall in Israel in 1983.*

mitzvah in Jerusalem at the Western Wall. Jesse was in his mid-teens by then, but he had not had a bar mitzvah at age thirteen as is customary. A widely circulated photograph showed the proud father wearing the skullcap and prayer shawl worn during prayer by traditional Jews.

Back in the United States, Dylan spent much time with a group of ultra-religious Orthodox Jews called Chabad Lubavitch. In addition, his next album, *Infidels*, included a song he wrote called "Neighborhood Bully," which was interpreted as a defense of Israel in its longtime struggle with its Arab neighbors.

What did Dylan have to say about all this? Nothing clear, as usual. To one reporter Dylan confessed that he had had no problem with his Christian preaching. But he added, "maybe the time for me to say that has come and gone. It's time for me to do something else. Sometimes those things appear quickly and disappear. Jesus himself only preached for three years."[10]

The legend began to come out of seclusion in March 1984, singing three songs on the television show *Late Night with David Letterman*. He followed with a lengthy tour of Europe, in which he appeared with Joan Baez again for two concerts in Germany.

A tragedy half a world away brought some of the world's best-known musicians together in an unlikely event. As a result of a civil war raging in the African nation of Ethiopia, millions there were starving to death. Bob Geldof, a member of the Irish rock group The Boomtown Rats, came up with a novel way to raise money. Late in 1984, he gathered together some of England's best-known bands to record a song titled, "Do They Know It's Christmas?" Money from sales of the record went to Ethiopian famine relief.

American musicians thought it was a wonderful idea and decided to record a similar song. In January 1985, Dylan and forty-five other artists recorded "We Are The World." Included with Dylan were some of music's hottest names including Bruce Springsteen, Stevie Wonder, Diana Ross, Billy Joel, and Michael Jackson. This multitude of musicians was called USA for Africa. USA had a double meaning, standing for the United States of America and also for United Support of Artists. "We Are The World" was a massive hit, reaching number one and staying at the top of the charts for four weeks that spring.[11]

Bob Geldof got together with two concert promoters to take this unusual charity event to the next level. On July 13, 1985, two rock concerts took place at the same time—one in London, the other in Philadelphia. Together, the twin concerts were known as Live Aid. Live Aid was televised for sixteen hours and featured rock's greatest artists. Phil Collins pulled off a tough feat; he played drums at the London concert, then flew a Concorde airplane across the Atlantic to play drums the same day in Philadelphia.

Dylan was given a position of honor, the last solo act in the Philadelphia show. He rendered old classics including "Blowin' in the Wind," accompanied by Keith Richards and Ron Wood of the Rolling Stones. Unfortunately, the sound equipment was not set up well and the quality was poor. But Live Aid was more about famine relief than a big party. The two concerts raised some $50 million to feed the starving.[12]

As might be expected, Dylan stirred up a bit of controversy. During his set, he suggested using some of the money raised during Live Aid to help American farmers. There was an economic crisis at the time affecting farmers in the United States. Many with farms in their families for generations could not afford to keep them. Dylan, being from a small Minnesota town and owner of his own farm, understood their problems.

Though Dylan's heart may have been in the right place, concert officials thought he stepped out of line. Americans may be losing their farms, but Africans were starving to death. Dylan seemed insensitive to the purpose of Live Aid.

Dylan's speech helped propel another charity concert to take place however. Popular country music singer Willie Nelson took Dylan's idea and ran with it. Nelson organized Farm Aid, with the purpose of helping American farmers pay off huge debts to keep their farms. The Farm Aid concert took place amid the soybean fields of Champaign, Illinois, on September 22, 1985. Dylan, Nelson, and other rock and country entertainers including Johnny Cash, Waylon Jennings, and Neil Young performed.

Dylan was as busy as ever. He released four albums in 1985 and 1986, including a five-record volume of fifty-three songs, including eighteen new ones. He also had a wedding in his future. Sometime-girlfriend Carolyn Dennis became pregnant with his child. Their daughter, Desiree Gabrielle Dennis-Dylan, was born on January 31, 1986. Dylan secretly married Carolyn on the following June 4. The marriage was kept private and this time word was not leaked to the media.

For the next few years, Dylan actively wrote songs, released albums and performed live. He also made another movie, called *Hearts of Fire*, in which he played a fictional music performer named Billy Parker. However, the movie was a disaster. It was first released in England where it received poor reviews and played for only a few weeks. It was never released in the United States. Then on January 20, 1988, Bob Dylan received what to many rockers is the ultimate honor—he was inducted into the Rock and Roll Hall of Fame.

# The President, the Pope, and the Chairman

A lot of rock-and-roll artists are well past their glory years when inducted into the Rock and Roll Hall of Fame. They may still perform, but their concerts are basically greatest hits shows. Fans want to hear the hits that made them famous, not their current projects.

At the time of Dylan's induction, he was starting to fall into that category. His new albums barely reached the top forty on the national chart and his solo concerts no longer filled huge stadiums. To draw a capacity crowd, Dylan had to co-star with another big act such as the Grateful Dead.

In the early spring of 1988, former Beatle George Harrison was in Los Angeles to make a quick record. Jeff Lynne, the project's producer, had once played guitar and keyboards with a British band called Electric Light Orchestra, which had had hits in the 1970s and early 1980s. Harrison and Lynne were looking for an inexpensive studio. Harrison recalled, "And the only studio we could find available was Bob's. So we thought Bob's got one, we'll just call him up."[1]

Lynne was also producing records for Tom Petty and Roy Orbison, one of rock music's pioneers who had several hits in the early 1960s. Petty and Orbison were invited to come along for the recording session. The talented quintet began jamming and writing new songs and decided to make them into an album. They called their impromptu group the Traveling Wilburys. Orbison said, "We all enjoyed it so much. It was so relaxed. There was no ego involved and there was some sort of chemistry going on."[2]

It was a time of personal changes for Dylan. In April 1989, he and Carolyn bought a new home. This was not in a glamorous town such as Malibu or Beverly Hills, but a Los Angeles suburb called Tarzana. No one would have expected to find Bob Dylan there, and he was determined to keep his and his family's privacy.

He appeared to be returning even more strongly to his Jewish roots by appearing with his son-in-law and an actor named Harry Dean Stanton at a Los Angeles fund-raiser for the Jewish religious group called Chabad. At the event, Dylan played the Jewish folk tune "Hava Nagila." Then on November 7, 1989, he became a grandfather for the first time. His stepdaughter

Maria and her husband, Peter, had a son they named Isaac.

There was another new addition to Dylan's legacy that fall. The album, *Traveling Wilburys Volume 1* was released and reached number three on the national album chart, higher than any solo Dylan album since *Slow Train Coming* nine years earlier.[3] Sadly, Roy Orbison did not live to see its success. He died of a heart attack on December 6, 1988, at age fifty-two. Dylan, Lynne, Petty, and Harrison released a second Traveling Wilburys album in October 1990. Although it was the group's second album, they jokingly titled it, *Traveling Wilburys Volume 3*, and it reached number 11.[4]

In the fall of 1990, the United States was on the brink of war against Iraq and there was a surge of patriotism in the country. The nation's mood was the polar opposite of the disruptive days of the Vietnam War. Whether it was intentional or not, Dylan played his first concert at a military academy in October. The setting was the United States Military Academy at West Point, New York. Who would have thought Bob Dylan, once so anti-military and anti-war, would be entertaining army cadets? But there he was.

On the verge of turning fifty, Dylan had become a senior statesman of rock music. The Grammy Awards honored him with a Lifetime Achievement Award on February 20, 1991. While accepting the honor, Dylan gave a bizarre speech. Standing at the podium, he looked ill. Some have said Dylan had the flu. Others have maintained he was drunk from once again abusing alcohol. On national television, Dylan stated,

"Well, my daddy, he didn't leave me much, you know he was a very simple man, but what he did tell me was this, he did say, 'son,' he said."

Dylan then paused for a long time, as if he forgot what he wanted to say. Uneasiness filled the hall. Some in the audience laughed nervously.

Dylan finished his thoughts, continuing, "he say, 'you know it's possible to become so defiled in this world that your own father and mother will abandon you and if that happens, God will always believe in your ability to mend your ways.'"[5]

Biblical experts recognized that Dylan's words were based on a verse from the Bible. Psalms, chapter 27, verse 10, reads: "For though my father and mother have forsaken me, The Lord will take me up."[6] It is recited by Jews during prayer services in the month before the Jewish New Year.

Dylan fans have since analyzed just what he meant that night. Did his father really say those words or did Dylan just make that up? Did he plan to say them that night or did the words just come out on the spur of the moment? And who was he referring to about becoming "defiled"? The music industry? People in general? Somebody specific in his life?

One Dylan biographer, Howard Sounes, wrote, "It seemed to many watching that Bob was talking about himself, meaning that his father would have been shocked by the state he was in if he could have been there to see him."[7]

When asked about it years later, Dylan admitted that he was "probably paraphrasing" his father's words.[8] He added that he was disappointed that

*Dylan performed at the 2001 Academy Awards. He was not in attendance, but was shown live via satellite from Australia where he was on tour.*

many musicians who said they would take part in Dylan's tribute canceled their appearances after the war against Iraq started. He said the speech was directed towards the music community in general, especially those who "can't at least be true to their word. I just lost all respect for them. . . . There are a few that are decent and God-fearing and will stand up in a righteous way. But I wouldn't want to count on most of them."[9]

To a lot of his fans, all that mattered was the man's music. A total of fifty-eight previously unreleased Dylan songs were packaged as *The Bootleg Series, Volumes 1-3* and released in March 1991. They sold moderately well, and were highly thought of by critics. The next year, Dylan marked three decades in the recording industry with a gala Thirtieth Anniversary Celebration concert in New York City's Madison Square Garden.

Soon afterwards, Dylan and his second wife, Carolyn, divorced. With Dylan on the road so often, they were rarely together. Their divorce took place as secretly as their wedding had.

Although no longer a chart topper, Dylan was invited to perform at high-profile events. In January 1993, he sang at the Lincoln Memorial as part of President Bill Clinton's first inauguration gala. In the summer of 1994 he finally performed at Woodstock. This was Woodstock '94, a concert celebrating the twenty-fifth anniversary of the groundbreaking first Woodstock concert that Dylan had snubbed.

That fall, Dylan showed that while he might be middle-aged, he was no rock-and-roll dinosaur. Music video cable network MTV invited him to sing as part of its "Unplugged series," where well-known music artists perform acoustically. On December 14 on MTV, Dylan sang most of his classics, and the concert was released as both a compact disc (CD) and video-tape. It was one of his highest-ranking albums in years, peaking at number 23 the following spring.[10]

It was also in the mid-1990s that some observers say that Dylan started taking better care of himself. However, Dylan denied having any alcohol problem. When told that some writers said he was drinking too much, Dylan responded, "That's completely inaccurate."[11] He explained his opinion of those writers.

"They might hear rumors. They might start rumors, but it's their own minds going to work."[12]

Regardless, it was clear that Dylan was morphing from one of rock's elder statesmen into a living legend. If an ambassador of rock music was needed, Dylan was called upon. This included some unlikely events, such as the eightieth birthday of Frank Sinatra. Known as "The Chairman of The Board," Sinatra, like Dylan, was another music legend. But he was from a different age, having become popular in the early 1940s during the big band era. To rock-and-roll fans, Sinatra represented their parents' tastes. Yet here they were together in 1995—Bob Dylan and Frank Sinatra, two music greats from different generations, side by side.

Then Dylan's name was raised in a place that years earlier would have been unheard of. A college professor named Gordon Ball, who taught English and fine arts at the Virginia Military Institute, nominated Dylan for the Nobel Prize for Literature. Ball wrote to the Nobel Academy, "Since the early 1960s Mr. Dylan in word and music has created an almost unlimited universe of art which has permeated the globe and in fact changed the history of the world."[13] Dylan did not win the singular honor, but the fact that he was nominated and taken seriously proved his acceptance by the mainstream.

Dylan turned fifty-six in 1997 and his daughter Maria arranged a small birthday party for the family. At the party, Maria noticed her father did not look well. A doctor diagnosed him with a condition called pericarditis, the result of a fungus infection. The condition caused a sac around his heart to inflame, and it could have been very serious, possibly fatal. Luckily, it was treated in time and Dylan was released from the hospital six days later. He joked about his brush with death, saying, "I really thought I'd be seeing Elvis soon."[14] (Elvis Presley had died in 1977.)

Though still weak and sometimes dizzy from his illness, Dylan worked on a new album to be called *Time Out of Mind.* He also toured that summer, and in September played for one of his most distinguished audiences. At an important religious meeting in Bologna, Italy, Dylan played for two hundred thousand fans including Pope John Paul II. The Pope sat to the side as Dylan sang several numbers including "Knockin' on Heaven's Door." After the set, the Pope referred to Dylan in a sermon. The seventy-seven-year-old Pope said to the young audience, "Just before, a representative of yours said on your behalf that the answer is blowing in the wind. Yes. It is true. . . . on the wind that is the voice and breath of the Spirit."[15]

Dylan's children were now adults but had managed to stay out of the public eye. The one exception was Jakob, who became a performer. In the early 1990s he formed a band called the Wallflowers. Their first album bombed, but their second album called *Bringing Down The Horse* was released in 1997 and was huge. To Jakob's credit, he did not take advantage of his family name for success. He was just one member of his band. On November 17, both the Wallflowers and Dylan were in San Jose, California, and father and son performed on the same bill.

The honors kept coming. On December 7, 1997, Bob Dylan received the esteemed Kennedy Center medal. President Clinton presided over the ceremony, and Dylan brought his eighty-two-year-old mother to sit by his side. It was probably the first time most people had seen Bob Dylan wearing a tuxedo.

Ten years earlier it appeared that Dylan would be one of those rock artists whose best days were in the past. But *Time Out of Mind* became Dylan's best selling album since *Slow Train Coming*. It reached number ten on the national album chart and stayed in the top one hundred for twenty-nine weeks.[16] At the Grammy Awards in February 1998, it won in three categories including "Album of the Year."

*In 1997, Dylan received the Kennedy Center Medal. President Bill Clinton presided over the ceremony.*

There were no cryptic messages in Dylan's acceptance speeches as there had been in 1992. He thanked his back-up musicians and reminisced about seeing one of rock's founding fathers, Buddy Holly, in 1959, perform live three days before a fatal airplane crash. In a touching tribute, Dylan referred to Holly by announcing, "I know he was with us all the time we were making this record in some way."[17]

It was a family affair that night. Jakob Dylan and his band the Wallflowers also won two awards for "One Headlight," their hit single from *Bringing Down the Horse.*

A reporter covering the event for *The New York Times* wrote, "at the 40th annual Grammy Awards ceremony, the Dylan name was a guaranteed winner."[18]

Bob Dylan is going strong. He continues to tour and record. Movies have made him even more visible. *Hurricane*, a feature film based on Hurricane Carter's life and starring Denzel Washington, drew many to the theaters in 2000. Included on the soundtrack was Dylan's 1975 song, "Hurricane." Then in 2001, Dylan won his first Academy Award, given by the movie industry, for his song "Things Have Changed." It was on the soundtrack of a movie called *The Wonder Boys*. And in May that year, online voters in Great Britain voted him the greatest lyricist of all time. He gathered 32.6 percent of the total vote. John Lennon was second with 18 percent.[19]

Even though Dylan was about to turn sixty, he was not free from controversy. In 2001, writer Howard Sounes released a bombshell in a Dylan biography he wrote. Sounes announced the news that Dylan had kept quiet for so long—that he was secretly married to Carol Dennis. Earlier books had always referred to Dennis as Dylan's girlfriend. Dennis confirmed publicly that Sounes was correct and declared, "Bob and I made a choice to keep our marriage a private matter for a simple reason—to give our daughter a normal childhood."[20]

On February 27, 2002, Dylan won another Grammy award. It was in the category of "Best Contemporary Folk Album" for Dylan's newest release, *Love and Theft*. Then on August 3, he performed at the Newport Folk Festival for the first time since his legendary appearance in 1965.

Under a fake wig and white cowboy hat and

*Bob Dylan still performs live. He is pictured here at a Nashville music festival in 2001.*

behind a false beard, Dylan rendered new numbers such as "Cry Awhile" and classics including "The Times They Are A-Changin'" and "Like a Rolling Stone." He performed both acoustically and electrically, and while there was no controversy this time, the Newport homecoming received mixed and poor reviews. One critic who had attended the infamous 1965 Newport show, Sheila Lennon, reported, "There was no magic in the music. We had never danced, not once."[21] Another reviewer, Daniel Gewertz, wrote, "And while there were a few fine moments, the show wasn't one of his stronger affairs."[22]

Then in December 2002 a fifth bootleg series of Dylan recordings was released. It was titled *Bob Dylan, The Bootleg Series: Vol. 5—Bob Dylan Live 1975: The Rolling Thunder Revue,* and included twenty-two tracks recorded during Rolling Thunder Revue performances in Massachusetts and Montreal. Included were classics such as "A Hard Rain's a-Gonna Fall," "The Lonesome Death of Hattie Carroll," and the then brand new "Hurricane." A critic for the national newspaper *USA Today* rated it three and a half stars out of four, reporting that "every track sizzles with an undercurrent of tension and reckless instinct."[23]

After years and years of performing, Newport 2002 and the fifth bootleg series proved that Bob Dylan was still a major player on the music scene The troubadour is over sixty, but still devoted to creating new songs and bringing renewed life to his old ones. Chances are likely Bob Dylan won't be quitting soon.

# Author's Note

Bob Dylan's grandfather was named Zigman Zimmerman. My great-grandfather was similarly named Moshe Zimmerman. Before immigrating to the United States, Zigman Zimmerman lived in the city of Odessa in the Ukraine. Before immigrating to the United States, Moshe Zimmerman lived in the city of Odessa in the Ukraine.

While in Odessa, Zigman Zimmerman worked in the shoe manufacturing business. Moshe Zimmerman also worked in the shoe business.

Zigman Zimmerman and Moshe Zimmerman were both practicing Jews, and both immigrated to ensure better lives for themselves and their families.

Zigman Zimmerman settled in Duluth, Minnesota, in 1907. Moshe Zimmerman settled in Hartford, Connecticut, sometime between 1903 and 1906. It was common for members of eastern European families to move to the United States over the course of several years, and our family's oral history tells of an ancestor who left Odessa to settle in the northern Midwest.

So it is not surprising that there has for sometime been in our family lore the story that the Schumans and Bob Dylan are related. We have never been able to verify a common ancestor, but we like to think proof is out there somewhere. For that reason, the Schumans have had a special interest in the life of Bob Dylan.

This book tells the story of one of the most talented persons in American entertainment history. And should we ever find the evidence that we are indeed related, I would certainly be proud to call Bob Dylan my cousin—even a distant one.

Then again, who wouldn't?

# Chronology

1941—Born Robert Allen Zimmerman in Duluth, Minnesota, on May 24.

1947—Moves with family to Hibbing, Minnesota.

1955—Sees movie *Rebel Without a Cause* which deeply influences him.

1958—Stirs up controversy with wild performance at high school talent show.

1959—Graduates high school.

1959 –1960—Attends University of Minnesota.

Around 1960—Changes stage name to Bob Dylan.

1960—Moves to Denver, Colorado.

Around late 1960–early 1961—Moves to New York City.

1961—Meets and befriends idol Woody Guthrie; first rave review in *The New York Times* on September 29; signs first recording contract with Columbia Records on October 26.

1962—First album, *Bob Dylan*, is released on March 19; legally changes name to "Bob Dylan" on August 9.

1963—Becomes hero to young people when he turns down chance to appear on national television over censorship issue; second album, *The Freewheelin' Bob Dylan*, released on May 27 and becomes first hit on national chart; first plays Carnegie Hall.

1964—Third album, *The Times They Are A-Changin'*, released in February; fourth album, *Another Side of Bob Dylan* is released in August, 1965; fifth album, *Bringing It All back Home*, is released in March; controversial appearance at Newport Folk Festival on July 25; single "Like A Rolling Stone" hits number 2; sixth album, *Highway 61 Revisited*, released in August; secretly marries Sara Lowndes on November 22.

1966—Son Jesse is born on January 6; moves to Woodstock, New York, in May; seventh album, the classic *Blonde on Blonde*, released in May; motorcycle accident in July spurs semi-retirement.

1967—Privately records *The Basement Tapes* with members of The Band June–October; daughter Anna is born July 11.

1968—*John Wesley Harding* is released in January; son Samuel is born July 30.

1969—*Nashville Skyline* released in April; plays Isle of Wight Festival August 31; son Jakob is born December 9.

1970—*Self Portrait* and *New Morning* are released; moves back to New York City.

1971—Celebrates thirtieth birthday in Israel; plays Bangladesh benefit concert.

1973—Movie *Pat Garrett and Billy the Kid*, and soundtrack album are released; first concert tour since motorcycle accident.

1974—*Planet Waves* becomes Dylan's first number one album.

1975—*The Basement Tapes* is released in July; single "Hurricane" is released in fall.

1975—Tours with Rolling Thunder Revue.
–1976

1977—Files for divorce from Sara on March 1.

1978—Movie *Renaldo and Clara* is released January 25; begins long world tour.

1979—Release of *Slow Train Coming* in August signals Dylan's conversion to Christianity.

1980—Wins first Grammy Award for "Gotta Serve Somebody."

1983—Releases *Infidels*, first album without Christian theme since *Slow Train Coming*; spends time with Orthodox Jewish religious group Chabad Lubavitch.

1985—Sings on "We Are The World"; plays Live Aid July 13; plays Farm Aid November 22.

1986—Daughter Desiree Gabrielle Dennis-Dylan is born on January 31; Dylan secretly marries Desiree's mother Carolyn Dennis on June 4.

1988—Inducted into Rock and Roll Hall of Fame.

1989—Album *Traveling Wilburys Volume I* is released and is a huge hit.

1991—Receives Lifetime Achievement Grammy Award at age forty-nine; *The Bootleg Series - Volumes 1-3* released in March; secretly divorces second wife, Carolyn.

1993—Performs at President Bill Clinton's inaugural ceremony.

1995—Album *MTV Unplugged* released.

1996—First nominated for Nobel Prize for Literature.

1997—Hospitalized with fungal infection; plays for Pope John Paul II in Italy; album *Time Out of Mind* is released; receives Kennedy Center honor on December 7.

1998—*Time Out Of Mind* sweeps Grammy awards.

2000—Feature film *Hurricane* is released, which includes Dylan's 1975 song of same name on soundtrack.

2001—Song "Things Have Changed" earns Dylan's his first Academy award.

2002—Plays Newport Folk Festival for the first time since controversial 1965 appearance.

## Selected Discography

### Albums and Compact Discs

*Bob Dylan* (Columbia, 1962)
*The Freewheelin' Bob Dylan* (Columbia, 1963)
*The Times They Are A-Changing'* (Columbia, 1964)
*Another Side Of Bob Dylan* (Columbia, 1964)
*Bringing It All Back Home* (Columbia, 1965)
*Highway 61 Revisited* (Columbia, 1965 )
*Blonde On Blonde* (Columbia, 1966)
*Bob Dylan's Greatest Hits* (Columbia, 1967)
*John Wesley Harding* (Columbia, 1968)
*Nashville Skyline* (Columbia, 1969)
*Self Portrait* (Columbia, 1970)
*New Morning* (Columbia, 1970)
*Bob Dylan's Greatest Hits, Vol. II* (Columbia, 1971)
*Pat Garrett & Billy The Kid* (Columbia, 1973)
*Planet Waves* (credited to Bob Dylan and The Band) (Asylum, 1974)
*Before The Flood* (credited to Bob Dylan and The Band) (Asylum, 1974)
*Blood On The Tracks* (Columbia, 1975)
*The Basement Tapes* (credited to Bob Dylan and The Band) (Columbia, 1975)
*Desire* (Columbia, 1976)
*Slow Train Coming* (Columbia, 1979)
*Saved* (Columbia, 1980)
*Shot of Love* (Columbia, 1981)
*Infidels* (Columbia, 1983)
*Empire Burlesque* (Columbia, 1985)

*Biograph* (Columbia, 1985)

*Traveling Wilburys, Vol. 1* (credited to The Traveling Wilburys) (Wilbury, 1988)

*Dylan & The Dead* (credited to Bob Dylan and The Grateful Dead) (Columbia, 1989)

*The Bootleg Series—Volumes 1-3* (Columbia, 1991)

*Traveling Wilburys, Vol. 3* (credited to The Traveling Wilburys) (Wilbury, 1990)

*Good As I Been To You* (Columbia, 1992)

*World Gone Wrong* (Columbia, 1993)

*Greatest Hits Volume 3* (Columbia, 1994)

*MTV Unplugged* (Columbia, 1995)

*Time Out Of Mind* (Columbia, 1997)

*The Bootleg Series Vol. 4—Live 1966* (Columbia, 1998)

*The Essential Bob Dylan* (Columbia, 2000)

*Love and Theft* (Columbia, 2001)

# Chapter Notes

## Chapter 1. Passing the Basket

1. "Playboy interview: Bob Dylan," originally published in February 1966 Playboy, reproduced in <www.interferenza.com/bcs/interw/66-jan.htm> (October 5, 2001).

2. Robert Shelton, "Bob Dylan: A Distinctive Folk-Song Artist," *The New York Times*, September 29, 1961, p. 31.

3. Clinton Heylin, *Bob Dylan: Behind the Shades Revisited*, (New York: William Morrow, 2001), p. 77.

## Chapter 2. The Rocking Golden Chords

1. Clinton Heylin, *Bob Dylan: Behind the Shades Revisited*, (New York: William Morrow, 2001), p. 7.

2. Robert Shelton, *No Direction Home: The Life and Music of Bob Dylan, July 3–9, 1978*, (New York: Beech Tree Books, 1986), p. 30.

3. Ibid., pp. 30–31.

4. "The Philippe Adler Interview: July 1978, <www.interferenza.com/bcs/interw/78-jul.htm> (October 6, 2001).

5. Shelton, p. 34.

6. Ibid., p. 35.

7. Johnny Ray home page, <www.johnnyray.com> (May 6, 2002).

8. Bob Spitz, *Dylan: A Biography*, (New York: Viking Penguin, Inc., 1989), p. 33.

## Chapter 3. Nights in Dinkytown

1. Robert Shelton, *No Direction Home: The Life and Music of Bob Dylan*, (New York: Beech Tree Books, 1986), p. 47.

2. Bob Spitz, *Dylan: A Biography*, (New York: Viking Penguin, Inc., 1989), p. 61.

3. Ibid.

4. Editors of *Memories* magazine, *Yearbook,* (New York: Dolphin, Doubleday, 1990), p. 107.

5. "The Philippe Adler Interview: July 1978," <www. interferenza.com/bcs/interw/78-jul.htm> (October 6, 2001).

6. "Playboy Interview: Bob Dylan," <www.interferenza. com/bcs/interw/66-jan.htm> (October 5, 2001).

7. Tim Riley, *Hard Rain: A Dylan Commentary* (New York: Alfred A. Knopf, 1992), pp. 18–19.

## Chapter 4. Meeting Woody

1. Bob Spitz:, *Dylan: A Biography,* (New York: Viking Penguin, Inc., 1989), p. 113.

2. Tim Riley, *Hard Rain: A Dylan Commentary* (New York: Alfred A. Knopf, 1992), p. 18.

3. Spitz, p. 114.

4. Ibid., p. 153.

## Chapter 5. Jammin' With Hammond's Folly

1. "October 1961, Billy James interview, New York City, New York," <http://youngbutdailygrowing.home. att.net/interviews/610929.01.html> (May 15, 2002).

2. Ibid.

3. Bob Spitz, *Dylan: A Biography,* (New York: Viking Penguin, Inc., 1989), p. 193.

4. Ibid.

5. Clinton Heylin, *Bob Dylan: Behind the Shades Revisited,* (New York: William Morrow, 2001), p. 116.

6. Joel Whitburn, *The Billboard Book of Top 40 Hits,* (New York: Billboard Publications, Inc., 1996), p. 468.

7. Ibid.

8. "'I Am My Words,'" *Newsweek,* November 4, 1963, p. 94.

9. Ibid., pp. 94–95.

10. Robert Shelton, *No Direction Home: The Life and Music of Bob Dylan* (New York: Beech Tree Books, 1986), p. 246.

11. Patrick Humphries and John Bauldie, *Absolutely Dylan: An Illustrated Biography*, (New York: Viking Studio Books, 1991), p. 178.

## Chapter 6. My Hands Are on Fire

1. Clinton Heylin, *Behind the Shades Revisited: Bob Dylan*, (New York: William Morrow, 2001), p. 165.

2. David Hajdu, *Positively 4th Street: The Lives and Times of Joan Baez, Bob Dylan, Mimi Baez Farina and Richard Farina* (New York: Farrar, Straus & Giroux, 2001), p. 203.

3. Joel Whitburn, *The Billboard Book of Top 40 Hits*, (New York: Billboard Publications, Inc., 1996), p. 196.

4. Robert Shelton, *No Direction Home: The Life and Music of Bob Dylan* (New York: Beech Tree Books, 1986), p. 300.

5. Dave Marsh, "Out of the 60's, Into His 50's," May 19, 1991, <www.nytimes.com/books/97/05/04/reviews/dylan-50.html> (June 21, 2002).

6. Whitburn, p. 196.

7. Shelton, p. 279.

8. Hajdu, p. 260.

9. "Dylan Goes Electric," July 25, 1965, <www.ew.com/ew/fab400/music100/3-4.html> (June 21, 2002).

10. Jac Holzman, Follow the Music excerpt. "Stuff You Don't Know About the 60s," "Dylan Goes Electric at Newport 1965," <www.followthemusic.com/60s.html> (June 21, 2002).

11. Hadju, pp. 260-261.

12. Holzman, "Stuff You Don't Know About the 60s," "Dylan Goes Electric at Newport 1965," <www.followthemusic.com/60s.html> (June 21, 2002).

13. Hadju, p. 263.

14. Thomas Meehan, "Public Writer No. 1?," December 12, 1965, <www.nytimes.com/books/97/05/04/reviews/dylan-writer.html> (June 21, 2002).

15. Ibid.

16. Whitburn, p. 95.
17. Ibid., p. 620.
18. Ibid., p.119.
19. Ibid., p. 235.

## Chapter 7. Cheating Death

1. Robert Shelton, "Dylan Conquers Unruly Audience," *The New York Times*, August 30, 1965, p. 20.

2. Ibid.

3. Joel Whitburn, *The Billboard Book of Top 40 Hits*, (New York: Billboard Publications, Inc., 1996), p. 196.

4. Bob Spitz:, *Dylan: A Biography*, (New York: Viking Penguin, Inc., 1989), p. 352.

5. "The Rolling Stone Interview," conducted by Jann Wenner, originally published November 29, 1969, in *Rolling Stone* magazine, <www.rollingstone.com/features/cs47article.asp> (October 5, 2001).

6. Clinton Heylin, *Behind the Shades Revisited: Bob Dylan*, (New York: William Morrow, 2001), p. 307.

7. Ibid.

8. Patrick Humphries and John Bauldie, *Absolutely Dylan: An Illustrated Biography*, (New York: Viking Studio Books, 1991), p. 199.

## Chapter 8. Catching the Eye of the Hurricane

1. Joel Whitburn, *Joel Whitburn's Top Pop Albums*, (Menominee Falls, Wisconsin: Record Research, Inc., 2001), p. 255.

2. Joel Whitburn, *The Billboard Book of Top 40 Hits*, (New York: Billboard Publications, Inc., 1996), p. 196.

3. Vincent Canby, "Screen: Peckinpah's 'Pat Garrett and Billy the Kid,'" *The New York Times*, May 24, 1973, p. 53.

4. Howard Sounes, *Down the Highway: The Life of Bob Dylan*, (New York: Grove Press, 2001), p. 274.

5. Joel Whitburn, *Joel Whitburn's Top Pop Albums*, p. 255.

6. Ibid.

7. Jim Jerome, "Bob Dylan: A Myth Materializes with a New Protest Record and a New Tour," originally published November 10, 1975, *People*, reproduced in <www.inter-ferenza.com/bcs/interw/75-nov10.htm> (October 5, 2001).

8. Neil Hickey, profile of Bob Dylan, originally published September 11, 1976, TV Guide, <www.interferenza.com/bcs/interw/76-sep11.htm> (October 5, 2001).

9. Joel Whitburn, *Joel Whitburn's Top Pop Albums*, p. 255.

10. Sounes, p. 292.

11. Ibid., p. 294.

12. "The Karen Hughes Interview in Sydney April 1, 1978," originally published in *Rock Express No. 4*, <www.interferenza.com/bcs/interw/78-apr1.htm> (October 6, 2001).

13. Janet Maslin, "'Renaldo and Clara,' Film by Bob Dylan," *The New York Times*, January 26, 1978, p. C18.

14. Sounes, p. 314.

## Chapter 9. Time for Me to Do Something Else

1. Larry Yudelson, "Dylan: Tangled Up in Jews," originally published in *Washington Jewish Week*, 1991, <www.radiohazak.com/Tangled.html> (October 5, 2001).

2. Joel Whitburn, *The Billboard Book of Top 40 Hits*, (New York: Billboard Publications, Inc., 1996), p. 196.

3. Joel Whitburn, *Joel Whitburn's Top Pop Albums*, (Menominee Falls, Wisconsin: Record Research, Inc., 2001), p. 255.

4. Henry Tiernan, "The Diamond Voice Within," originally published in *New Musical Express*, August 15, 1981, pp. 29-31, <www.interferenza.com/bcs/interw/81-aug15.htm> (October 6, 2001).

5. Joel Whitburn, *Joel Whitburn's Top Pop Albums*, p. 255.

6. Howard Sounes, *Down the Highway: The Life of Bob Dylan*, (New York: Grove Press, 2001), p. 335.

7. Tiernan.

8. Sounes, pp. 337–338.

9. Joel Whitburn, *Joel Whitburn's Top Pop Albums,* p. 255.

10. Robert Shelton, *No Direction Home: The Life and Music of Bob Dylan* (New York: Beech Tree Books, 1986), p. 488.

11. Joel Whitburn, *The Billboard Book of Top 40 Hits,* p. 625.

12. Shelton, p. 494.

## Chapter 10. The President, the Pope, and the Chairman

1. <www.wilburys.info/instrav.html> "How It All began." (June 6, 2002).

2. <www.wilburys.info/quotes.html> "Quotes," (June 6, 2002).

3. Joel Whitburn, *Joel Whitburn's Top Pop Albums,* (Menominee Falls, Wisconsin: Record Research, Inc., 2001), p. 892.

4. Ibid.

5. Ronnie Schreiber, "Dylan's Grammy Acceptance Speech Explicated," <www.radiohazak.com/Tangled.html> (October 5, 2001).

6. *The Holy Scriptures,* (The Jewish Publication Society of America: Philadelphia, 1955), p. 883.

7. Howard Sounes, *Down the Highway: The Life of Bob Dylan,* (New York: Grove Press, 2001), p. 395.

8. Mikal Gilmore, "Bob Dylan," *Rolling Stone,* November 22, 2001, p. 63.

9. Ibid.

10. Joel Whitburn, *Joel Whitburn's Top Pop Albums,* p. 256.

11. Gilmore, p. 64.

12. Ibid.

13. "Bob Dylan—finally and formally launched as a candidate for the Nobel Prize for Literature, 1997," press release, <www.expectingrain.com/dok/art/nobel/Nobelpress.html> (June 11, 2002).

14. "Bob Dylan Released From Hospital Treatment Continues and Full Recovery Expected," Sony Music press release, June 2, 1997, <www.edlis.org/twice/threads/dylan_hospitalization_update.html> (June 11, 2002).

15. Andrea Orlandi, "The Show 27/9," <www.interferenza.com/bcs/itpope.htm> (June 11, 2002).

16. Joel Whitburn, *Joel Whitburn's Top Pop Albums*, p. 246.

17. Jon Pareles, "Dylans, Father and Son, Gather Grammies; Shawn Colvin wins for 'Sunny', *The New York Times*, February 26, 1998, p. B9.

18. Ibid.

19. "Dylan 'the greatest songwriter,'" May 23, 2001, <http://news.bbc.co.uk/hi/english/entertainment/music/newsid_1347000/1347071.stm> (June 21, 2002).

20. "Dylan's Game of Hide and Seek," April 12, 2001, <http://more.abcnews.go.com/sections/entertainment/DailyNews/dylandaughter010412.html> (June 21, 2002).

21. Sheila Lennon, "Recital at Newport," Providence Journal website, http://www.projo.com/cgi-bin/include.pl/music/lennon_080402.htm> (August 4, 2002).

22. Daniel Gewertz, "Dylan doesn't think twice at Newport return," *Boston Herald*, <http://www2.bostonherald.com/entertainment/music/dyla08042002.htm>, (August 4, 2002).

23. Edna Gunderson, "'90s 2Pac raps again; '70s Dylan rocks again," *USA Today*, December 3, 2002, p. 6D.

# Further Reading

Dick, Arthur. *Play Guitar with Bob Dylan*. London, U.K.: Omnibus Press, 2001.

Dylan, Bob. *Bob Dylan Anthology: 50 More Songs from the Pen of One of This Generation's Most Distinct and Elpquent Voices*. New York: Music Sales Porporations, 1996.

Feinstein, Barry, Daniel Kramer and Jim Marshall. *Early Dylan*. Boston MA.: Little, Brown & Company, 1999.

Graham, Paul. *Dylan*. Upper Saddle River, N.J.: Prentice Hall, 2000.

Heylin, Clinton. *Dylan: Behind the Shades: The Biography*. City: Morrow, William & Company, 2001.

Richardson, Susan. *Bob Dylan*. Broomall, PA.: Chelsea House Publishers, 1995.

Sounes, Howard, *Down the Highway: The Life of Bob Dylan*. City: Grove Press, 2001.

# Internet Addresses

**Bob Dylan's official web site**
<http://www.bobdylan.com>

**Folk Music Archives**
<http://folkmusicarchives.org>

**Rock and Roll Hall of Fame**
<http://www.rockhall.com>

# Index

**I**

Israel, 63–64, 78–79

**J**

John Paul II, Pope, 90

**L**

Lennon, John, 43, 48, 60, 77–78, 92
Little Richard, 18–19, 23, 24, 25, 55
Live Aid, 80–81
Lois, George, 68–69
Lowndes, Sara, 47, 52, 57, 70, 72

**M**

Malibu, California, 64, 67, 84

**N**

Newport Folk Festival, 44–45, 49, 49–50, 53–54, 56, 93

**O**

Odetta, 27, 28

**P**

Peckinpah, Sam, 65
Peter, Paul and Mary, 42, 44

**R**

Ray, Johnny, 16
Rotolo, Suze, 34–35, 41–42, 46–47
Rubin, Judy, 20, 25, 28-29

**S**

Shelton, Robert, 7, 35, 52, 56, 60
Sinatra, Frank, 65, 89

**T**

Traveling Wilburys, 84

**W**

Wallflowers, The, 90, 92
Williams, Hank, 16, 41
Woodstock, New York, 62, 63, 67

**Z**

Zimmerman, Abram, 10–14, 21, 45
Zimmerman, Beatrice (Beatty), 11–14, 45, 70
Zimmerman, David Benjamin, 12, 20
Zimmerman, Robert Allen, *see* Dylan, Bob

PROPERTY OF
Kankakee Public Library